Happy Children

THROUGH POSITIVE PARENTING

Elizabeth Hartley-Brewer

Vermilion

LONDON

1 3 5 7 9 10 8 6 4 2

First published as *Positive Parenting* in the United Kingdom
in 1994 by Vermilion

This revised and updated edition published in the
United Kingdom in 2005 by Vermilion,
an imprint of Ebury Publishing
Random House UK Ltd.
Random House
20 Vauxhall Bridge Road
London SW1V 2SA

Random House Australia (Pty) Limited
20 Alfred Street, Milsons Point, Sydney,
New South Wales 2061, Australia

Random House New Zealand Limited
18 Poland Road, Glenfield,
Auckland 10, New Zealand

Random House (Pty) Limited
Endulini, 5A Jubilee Road, Parktown 2193, South Africa

Random House UK Limited Reg. No. 954009
www.randomhouse.co.uk
Papers used by Vermilion are natural, recyclable products
made from wood grown in sustainable forests.

A CIP catalogue record is available for this book from
the British Library.

ISBN: 0091902487

Printed and bound in Great Britain by
Cox and Wyman Ltd, Reading, Berkshire

For Stephen, Georgia, Julia and Greg

Contents

Acknowledgements

My first thanks go to those patient and tolerant friends and members of my family on whom I inflicted my earliest thoughts and developing ideas, and who gave me further insights. Many people acted as a sounding board, but the book would not have been written without the particular encouragement and continuing support of my sisters and mother.

I would also like to thank Alison Samuel, who provided sound advice on approaching publishers. Joan Freeman and David Hill willingly read the manuscript and made very helpful comments. Needless to say, responsibility for the content lies entirely with me.

Finally, I have to thank my immediate family, who endured sharing their lives with the ever-present 'book'. I have learnt a great deal from them; I hope they forgive me my mistakes.

Preface to the 2005 Edition

This book was first published just over ten years ago, under the title *Positive Parenting: Raising children with self-esteem*. Revisiting it to prepare this revised edition offered no surprises, as I have referred to it constantly throughout that time. Most of my subsequent books have developed particular themes first raised here, and for each one I began the project by rereading the relevant section or chapter. I have also considered it vital that I 'walk the talk' – that I behave to my own children as I recommend to others – so there have been times when I have referred to it for my own benefit. What I have to say in this book is a personal statement of my beliefs about what really matters in relationships with children. It represents the distillation of twenty-five years of trial and error, observation and contemplation – growing alongside first my two stepchildren and then my own two children; of working with gifted children and their families; and of sharing experiences with a large number of other mothers, fathers and friends – sometimes singly and sometimes in groups. I still consider that it identifies and summarises in a very useful way the fundamentals of children's needs and the common patterns of relationship that develop between parent and child; there is nothing central that I have wanted to change.

However, time alters the context. Ideas that were once new become accepted so need less justification or explanation, and issues seen initially as less significant become more pressing so require a stronger emphasis. For example, when this book was first written the importance of nurturing self-esteem in growing children as opposed to adults was hardly acknowledged; now it is widely accepted and has become the focus for many recent educational and social initiatives concerning children's achievement, inclusion and well-being. And ten years ago 'parenting' had no political profile, hence the references in the original conclusion to government responsibilities. Another big change is that divorce and separation now affects more children at a younger age, whether it be the ending of their own parents' relationship or that of a parent and subsequent live-in partner or legal step-parent. In addition, more mothers are returning to work when children are younger. I have therefore extended the final chapter to give greater emphasis to children's need to believe they have a continuing commitment from both parents despite any changed living arrangements or competing responsibilities at work. I have also drawn from up-to-date research and my own developing understanding to add one or two further thoughts to the sections on play, praise and physical punishment.

This book has already stood the test of time. I hope that its new format and emphases will engage a new generation of parents and help them to work through the inevitable pressures so they may enjoy a happy, positive and well-balanced relationship with their child.

Introduction

Children – like adults – perform best when they feel good about themselves. And they feel good about themselves when someone tells them they have done well, are likeable and are good to be with. Only when a child is convinced that her parents love, like and cherish her, and are on her side, can she develop true self-esteem and go on to become a self-confident, self-reliant and happy person.

This is a child-rearing book with a difference. It does not specify how and when to potty-train, when to move your toddler into a bed, or when to introduce solid food. There are many excellent books on such detailed and practical matters. It concentrates instead on understanding the ups and downs of the parent–child relationship and how to maintain a positive dynamic. It contains two simple core messages: first, trust yourself and your own instincts; and second, it is not so much *what you do* as *how you do it* that is important. Getting the approach right is much easier than most parents would believe. Once you realise that doing the best for your child and helping him to be relaxed, happy and outgoing comes down to creating in him self-esteem, self-confidence and self-reliance, the options become far clearer. And it is surprisingly easy to help your child have these 'self' qualities. The key things to remember can be related to the word *expertise*, using it as a memory jogger. This is explained in Chapter Five.

Readers should be buoyed and encouraged by what they read. This is because, no matter how many mistakes you have made in the past over how long a period, it offers a clear way forward. You can put the past behind you, forget guilt and apply this programme. It is, essentially, a valuable *tool kit*. But it can also act as a *repair kit* for anyone who feels they have lost all sense of direction and belief in their parental talents and even in themselves because their child's seemingly outrageous behaviour has pushed them to their limits. This can happen all too easily.

They should also feel empowered rather than intimidated and guilty. The book hands the initiative back to you, the parent. It says that everyone makes mistakes, that you can do it and that you don't need a continuous supply of experts or books. The expertise lies within you. You should rediscover and use the natural authority that you have as a parent. You should trust your own ability to decide what is the right thing to do, provided you have paid attention to the three targets – self-esteem, self-confidence and self-reliance. Immediately, your own self-esteem should improve and a virtuous circle can begin.

WHAT IS THE BOOK'S MESSAGE?

This book focuses on that essential ingredient of deeper happiness, self-esteem: what it is; why it is important to have it; what can go wrong if you don't have it; and, most important, how you can help your children to develop it. Unfortunately, people still seem to find it easier to do others down – to criticise, belittle and reject – rather than to approve, praise and enjoy.

After thirty years of being an active mother and a stepmother and learning from the inevitable mistakes; of reflecting on the behaviour of adults and the likely source of their difficulties; and, more recently, of working with groups of professionals and parents to develop a better understanding of child-rearing issues and parenting styles, I firmly believe that these three attributes – self-esteem, self-confidence and self-reliance – are the starting points for emotional health, happy relationships and a sense of satisfaction and the ability to commit to others in later life.

Self-esteem and the personal qualities that tend to accompany it are now widely accepted as important attributes for both adults and children. Positive self-esteem helps people be sensitive to the needs of others – sometimes described as emotional intelligence. It avoids the need to pretend because you are content to face the world as you are; it is also known to protect against depression and other forms of mental difficulty. Sound self-belief and self-esteem also help children to be resilient in the face of difficulties – to emerge from these a stronger, more reflective person. Lack of self-esteem is increasingly accepted as the reason why some young people fail to do themselves justice at school, succumb to anxiety and eating disorders and get into early trouble with the law; and why some undeniably successful children and adults none the less self-destruct. Although some people try to blame self-esteem for causing, as they see it, the increased selfishness, indulgence and lawlessness among children, they misunderstand its true nature – nurturing self-esteem and happiness does not mean giving in to every whim and letting children do whatever they want; quite the opposite. Few deny, though, that the roots of an enduring happy and positive outlook lie in childhood, and so it makes a great deal of sense to explore in detail what makes the difference and how we as parents can help our children to thrive.

A confident and happy disposition based on positive self-esteem is the best gift any parent can give their child.

Your own self-esteem is important too. It is vital to look after yourself alongside your child, to enable you to 'grow' and maintain your own feelings of competence and self-esteem rather than put yourself into cold storage for the duration. If you feel low and inadequate, you are far less likely to help your child to flourish. Using the guidance on how to help your child feel good about herself, and inviting you to apply some of it to yourself as well as to your child, the book asks you to believe in yourself: to trust your instincts; trust your ability to do the job successfully; reclaim your authority; and rediscover and trust your common sense.

Of course, the context of parenting matters a great deal as well. It is only natural that stress should hinder a parent's best efforts to keep calm and cool, and the long-hours working culture and family change and reformation can combine to make it hard to meet everyone's demands. It is all too easy to be sharp and hurtful rather than measured when under pressure and it may therefore be tempting to rely on strict routines to keep everyone and everything manageable. Although we know that children find life easier and feel more secure when they recognise predictable patterns that structure their day, there are dangers in returning to rigid, inflexible practices that ignore children's moods and sensitivities and prevent even babies from being listened to and respected. The latest research on how babies' and young children's brains develop shows the essential value of warmth, affection, intimate and responsive communication and the avoidance of distress from the very beginning. This is essential if children are to grow up with the part of their brain that controls and reads emotions fully developed and attuned. The research provides further evidence that emotional experiences in infancy and early childhood have a measurable effect on how we develop as human beings: in other words, child-sensitive, positive, authoritative and responsive but 'patterned' parenting is far more beneficial to children's all-round development than strictly ordered, highly rigid and disciplined practices.

This is a practical handbook – not a detailed route map that provides the answer to every issue on the sometimes rocky road of parenthood. It is, instead, more a guide to map-reading, letting you choose a route that suits you, having suggested some appropriate destinations and clear ground rules as to what makes a child feel secure, valued, wanted and happy. Everybody is different: you as a parent or carer have your individual personality, strengths and weaknesses, as does your child, so there can be no uniform answer to any situation. You have to discover what works for you, making the inevitable and necessary mistakes along the way. Provided that you keep in mind the key targets and strive to avoid putting your child down, a key message from this book is: it's OK to do it *your* way. The focus on promoting self-esteem and happiness is no longer new, and many parents will already be 'on board', either intuitively or through choice. What is not so common is having a coherent framework available against which to assess sensible responses to most of the issues that arise throughout childhood, and one which can also highlight the unintended consequences of some of our clumsy words and actions.

Thinking about all these issues will help us to:

- identify our own values
- accept responsibility for guiding and leading our children into adulthood according to those values
- provide us and our children with an authoritative sense of direction
- avoid the extremes of child-rearing fashion and identify a more sustainable middle way

HOW TO USE THE BOOK

Simple ideas are usually best presented in a simple way, and this is what I have attempted to do.

Chapter One looks at how, despite the special difficulties facing parents today, there is a way through which can rebuild our confidence and trust in ourselves.

Chapters Two and Three, 'The Tool Kit' and 'The Repair Kit', present an outline of the approach in a way which I hope is easy to understand. From then on, the book is 'layered'. In other words, the further you read into it, the deeper you can delve, moving beyond the core points and into some of the more complex dynamics of the parent–child relationship.

Chapter Four looks at where we, as parents, fit in. You could stop reading here and, I hope, still come out with some useful ideas.

Chapter Five introduces the key words, which not only reinforce and distil the main message but also act as memory-joggers. The words on their own say quite a lot, and each is followed by a short section which expands on the concept being presented, starting with the main points and going on to consider them in more detail. Each key word applies equally to the parent and to the child. Each section is therefore split into two, looking first at how the word relates to the child's needs, and then how it relates to those of the parent(s). You can read as much or as little as you want to here too.

Chapter Six, 'Words Matter', is for those who want to read and consider further still. It shows in more detail how and why we use words to put children down, and suggests other ways of saying things that are less hurtful.

Chapters Seven and Eight explore alternative discipline styles, the complexities of power and the importance of consistency and commitment in parenting, and how these can combine to influence self-esteem.

Chapter Nine summarises what is meant by 'positive parenting' in the positive and negative behaviour circles, which illustrate the cumulative effect of parental attitudes and actions on the child.

Some repetition is inevitable. Writing the book in this way, I try to allow different people to take what they want from it; and also to reinforce, progressively, the ideas and their importance.

A simple truth can also be profound, as I hope I shall show.

One final word: don't be deterred by the number of suggestions for action. They are not all meant to be tried, and certainly not all of them at one go. The examples are offered more for illustration than direction. As is suggested in Chapter Three, when you ask yourself at the end of the day what you have done to make your child feel secure, successful, important to you and thereby good about herself and you answer with more positives than negatives, that is good enough.

1

Trust Yourself:

IT'S OK TO DO IT *YOUR* WAY

Being a parent today is much harder than it was even ten years ago. There are several reasons why this is so.

Society is changing fast. Many people feel they have no coherent or relevant model for bringing up children in the twenty-first century. Today's parents will have come mostly from the smaller families more typical of recent times. While small families often provide greater material comforts and emotional benefits, the older children are usually so close in age to the younger ones that they either cannot, or are not needed to, help bring up or mind their much younger brothers or sisters. They therefore gain no early experience of child care which can be applied later with their own children – an experience which most world cultures offer. At the same time, and partly as a result of the same trend, the extended family is not there to play the guiding or supporting role that it used to.

Many more people today are parenting alone, for a wide variety of reasons. The decisions and lifestyle changes this entails are so significant that they will inevitably cause some measure of stress and anxiety. Children make big demands, either directly, or indirectly through poor behaviour. Unsettling changes will increase those demands as they seek reassurance. If there is only one parent to meet these sometimes intense demands, the pressure will be that much more concentrated.

These social changes are happening in a context that puts even more strain on parents. Today we live in a climate of 'professionalism'. Having lost confidence in ourselves, not only do we look increasingly to professionals to give us the answers to each and every one of our problems, but we also have ever higher personal standards and expect to be successful in all spheres. That is asking for too much. We cannot be superhuman and achieve excellence in all that we touch. When we inevitably fail, we are prone not just to guilt but also to further feelings of inadequacy and incompetence. Women especially can demand far too much of themselves.

In addition to this, many parents are trying to function in an authority void. In rejecting (rightly) the strict disciplinarian method of bringing up children, some parents have thrown away their authority and responsibility at the same time. Others have just lost their sense of direction and confidence in themselves. Someone who is confused and unsure will not command authority. Those who have consciously rejected the adult control which they themselves experienced in childhood in favour of a more child-centred approach now seem equally uncertain as to whether this alternative really works or gives children the best tools for coping and fitting in with the demands of education, work and family made on them later.

In the area of parenting, the relevant professionals are also telling us that what we do in these early years can have a big impact on the later personality of our child. This makes us increasingly anxious about making mistakes. Mothers are particularly prone to this type of anxiety. Believing it is our key job to provide our families with health and happiness, we worry not only about doing the job well, but also about the risk of causing psychological damage to our children.

And even that is not all. The state of marriages and partnerships is another pressure on us. We are all now constantly exposed to the expectation that we should have a high-quality sexual, emotional and social relationship with our partners and be 'happy'. The growing social accept-ability of divorce and single parenthood seduces us into weighing up the state of our relationships more frequently, because if we judge that we do not have an ideal relation-ship, we have the option to abandon ship, get out and find something better elsewhere. With that possibility always hanging over both partners in the relationship, even if it is subconscious, men and women are having to bring up their children in a potentially explosive environment of insecu-rity and failure in which we demand too much and see too little. We are in danger of ignoring the obvious. Not only can we undervalue ourselves – our instincts and abilities – but worse, we can fail to realise, as we try to square the circle of modern life, that our children have basic needs too that we ignore at their and our peril.

Just as adults perform best when they feel good about themselves and when others have shown they appreciate, love and care for them, so do children. A confident, trusting child, secure in her key relationships and conscious of her particular abilities and what it is that makes her unique, will play better, learn better, concentrate better and give, love and relate better. A child's sense of self develops from infancy. Therefore feelings about self-esteem, both good and bad, exist in childhood as strongly as, or indeed more strongly than, they do in adulthood. Good self-esteem helps people to develop strong self-confidence. Self-confidence helps people become self-reliant and independent. These three attributes combine in individuals regardless of age to create human beings who are happy, productive, creative, flexible and, most important when considering the social context of our lives, giving.

These qualities lie at the heart of almost everything people say they want for themselves. Childhood is by far the best time to build self-esteem, self-confidence and self-reliance. If they are not acquired then, it is far harder to adopt them as permanent features of yourself later. Where adults have relationship problems at home or at work, it is these qualities that they have often lacked. Where adults have other kinds of problems and they are not handling them well, it is usually because their resilience and belief in themselves is low.

If you think of learning as human building blocks, these 'self' perceptions go down first and constitute a person's foundations. With strong foundations, we can weather the storms and earthquakes of life. Without them, we bend, creak, heave and crack. We can repair the cracks; but if the foundations are weak, the cracks will only reappear. What this book sets out to do is show ways of laying these foundations.

As parents, if we want to find out how to be successful in our role, we need look no further than helping our children to develop confidence, self-reliance and, above all, good feelings about themselves. In terms of giving our children life-long advantages, anything else pales into insignificance.

Other decisions in parenting, if they cannot be related to these objectives, are far less important. They are not worth getting fussed about. It matters far more that you:

- keep the parent–child relationship alive and on an even keel
- maintain a consistent and predictable emotional and physical environment for your children
- keep power play and damaging disputes to a minimum
- demonstrate your unswerving commitment to them and show them that you understand them and are on their side

There is no formula for being the perfect parent and it is, in any case, an unrealisable dream. We all have times when pressures mean we don't cope so well. There are no easy answers, and you will not find a convenient blueprint here. Success is much more about understanding and trusting yourself and your children, and bringing them up *your way*, consistently. You know your children better than anyone else can or does. You are able to do it, not because you are clever or good at it, not because you know the theory or the tricks, but because your children are yours. By showing that you understand them as only you can, by respecting their likes and dislikes and acknowledging their strengths and weaknesses which make them who they are, by treating them with the respect that we should all give to each other as human beings and demonstrating that you approve of them, you will help them to grow up with a strong sense of themselves and a capacity for joy and fun, making them better able to withstand life's difficulties and to exploit life's challenges.

What we have to watch out for are the two demons: doubt and guilt. These are the most destructive elements of any relationship. They are especially the enemies of a natural and fulfilled relationship with children, both because they reinforce your uncertainty and insecurity and because they tempt you into an unhelpful regime of appeasement, or giving in. If we give in too often, we blur the boundaries. We teach our children that if they play on our guilt, they get their way. A small amount of guilt is healthy, but too much is definitely counterproductive. We all do make mistakes – through our over-concern, through stress or marital and relationship problems, through having to meet other family needs which often conflict. It is all right to make mistakes. If you can accept that you can mess things up, and the sky does not fall in when it happens, you will teach your children by example that it is also safe for them to make mistakes. If, on the other hand, you get crushed with a sense of failure, you teach them that making mistakes is something shameful and therefore to be avoided at all costs. Being able to take risks, and to accept both the possibility of and the responsibility for making mistakes, is an absolute prerequisite for learning and healthy development.

Some of our mistakes are minor and do not matter. Others can cause temporary harm or hurt. But there are two vital things to remember that should relieve the agony of guilt. One is that, in the vast majority of parent–child relationships, you can make amends and undo the mistake even quite a long time afterwards – so great is a child's need to be loved, trusted and respected by you – by apologising to them and repairing their self-image, which has been damaged as a result. For years and years they can be the most forgiving creatures. They have to rely on you, so they want and need to believe in you.

The second vital thing is that if you are unpleasant to children, and have not seriously hurt them emotionally or physically, there is in place a cushion of love, a suspension of judgement, and so strong a wish, or need, to believe in you that they and their relationship with you can take several knocks without significant damage. The danger only comes when that reserve of giving you the benefit of the doubt is used up. Then, to protect themselves from the uncomfortable conclusion that they are not worth loving, they separate themselves from you emotionally and are no longer willing to play any part in a relationship that exposes them to such anguish. This is what Bruno Bettelheim, the eminent child psychologist, and D.W. Winnicott, a paediatrician and psychoanalyst, meant when they talked about being a 'good enough' mother or parent. Provided you are not near the danger point, and you have loved your children in a way that has convinced them of it, there is room for error and repair, repeatedly.

So, trust yourself. You and your children have a unique relationship. And they adore you, love you and need you more than you can know. No one else can take your place as their mother or father. This is the fundamentally encouraging reality. Each relationship has to be not only different but also unique. You are you, with all of your strengths and weaknesses which you carry with you; and the child has her own unique personality from day one, which can be influenced but not changed without damaging her spirit. You have to work with what you have collectively got. Quite apart from that, there are partners and siblings who will alter the chemistry of what's possible to do within your family. No one can tell you precisely what will work for you two or even, at a more complex level, what will work within the whole family – taking other family members' values and boundaries or tolerances into account. Only you can know all this and put it into the equation of compromise. The answer does not lie out there in an encyclopaedia. It lies, and has to lie, within ourselves. You have to work out what works for you. And what works for you is OK. If it is working, don't listen to anyone else telling you that you should be doing it differently. If it is working without you behaving like a dictator and your child does not have significant problems of bad or anxiety-driven behaviour, it is probably working because you are getting the essentials right – giving your child love, respect and security. The finer details are less important.

But the essentials do matter. This book presents these as a tool kit, and summarises the necessary techniques through the scheme of 'The Expertise' in Chapter Five. It shows you how to *get* 'The Expertise', and *forget* the guilt.

2

Building a Firm Foundation:

I THE TOOL KIT

SELF-ESTEEM, SELF-CONFIDENCE AND SELF-RELIANCE

All parents want the best for their child, and they also start out wanting to do the best for their child. That is why many people, on becoming parents for the first time, head for the bookshops, libraries or magazine racks to find out how to do it. Unfortunately, babies do not come with instructions.

Wanting the best

Most parents would agree that the most important thing they want for their child is happiness. But what brings happiness? Different people will have very different ideas about this. Many will see happiness as something you feel as a result of some other desirable situation. Therefore, when parents are asked the question: 'What do you want for your children as they grow up?', they are more likely to answer, 'To do well', 'Not to want for anything', 'To have plenty of toys to play with', or 'To keep themselves busy'. When asked about the longer term, when their children have become independent adults, the answers will be along the lines of 'Success', 'To be well thought of', 'To have plenty of money', 'To get married and have children', 'To have an interesting life' and so on. We tend to think partly in terms of things which would bring us as individuals a sense of achievement, assuming that achievement in itself brings happiness; and partly in terms of activities which would make us, as parents, feel proud of our children. Parents also, commonly, have ambitions for their children that avoid the mistakes they feel they have made in their own lives. They want their children to 'better themselves' or 'not to do as I did'. By encouraging their children to achieve, in whatever terms they define, they think they are fulfilling their duty to deliver happiness. But are they? Is happiness something that parents have within their power to give to their children?

True happiness, it has been said, is not a place of arrival; it is a manner of travelling. If happiness is seen as something that you have to go out and find or buy, and can arrive at, by the same token it can also disappear. That kind of acquired happiness certainly exists but it is, by definition, external, transient and fragile. There is a deeper-rooted, more permanent happiness to be experienced which is internal. Whether or not you have it depends upon how comfortable you are with yourself. This is self-esteem. 'Happiness is Self-Contentedness' wrote the Greek philosopher Aristotle some three hundred years before the birth of Christ.

Parents can and do have a major influence over whether their children possess or experience self-contentedness.

Being pushy and asking for more than their children can comfortably deliver won't help; neither will identifying with their failures and making them feel responsible for any intense disappointment. Doing the best for your children means helping them to experience a robust self-worth and self-belief gained through the development of self-confidence and self-reliance.

SELF-ESTEEM

What is self-esteem?

Self-esteem relates to:
- self-image
- self-contentedness
- self-acceptance
- self-worth
- self-approval

Self-esteem means feeling good about yourself. It means liking yourself and being content with, and even proud of, who you are. If you have self-esteem, you are happy to be you and you believe in your intrinsic value as a unique individual. It therefore involves having a positive self-image and an accurate self-awareness. You know who you are, and you can accept who you are without fear, embarrassment or doubt because you accept all of it. You like enough of yourself to be able to live with the bits that you find less endearing. If you know you are good at some things, it helps you acknowledge, without any loss to your self-image, that you are not so good at other things. Acknowledging both weak and strong points helps you to open up your whole self to the world outside. Nothing needs to be hidden or suppressed. Self-esteem is also self-sustaining. It is like having an electrical generator inside. When you feel low, or run down, you can recharge your own batteries. People without good self-esteem find it much harder to do this on their own. They need another power source to recharge them. They may find this in other people, or in challenging situations that give them a transient sense of achievement. People with poor self-esteem are constantly on the lookout for the source of their next power fix. If they are feeling *really* low, they will not even allow others near enough to 'refuel' them, and they sometimes end up throwing themselves away as a spent force.

Good self-esteem, therefore, is liberating, calming, regenerating and self-sustaining.

Why is it important to develop good self-esteem?

Self-esteem helps to give us:
- happiness
- resilience
- creativity
- the ability to take risks
- flexibility and adaptability
- the ability to give and commit to others
- common sense

If you are *resilient*, you do not go to pieces when faced with difficult and unexpected challenges. You can offer help and stability to others when they need support. Life is full of disappointments and difficulties. If we can give our children the tools and attributes to survive knocks and to bounce back, we will have given them something of life-long value.

If you are *creative*, you have the ability to think of different ways to manage situations. You are a problem-solver, not a problem-builder. Being able to see your way round and through problems is a great advantage. Problem-builders do not get very far, and they may find that their friends and acquaintances soon tire of their negative attitudes.

If you are *able to take risks*, you can try new things without being frightened of failing or of not being able to manage unforeseen events. This means you can go on learning, discovering and developing yourself to your life's end.

If you can be *flexible and adaptable*, you will be able to sustain longer and more rewarding relationships, enjoy the unknown, use what you know in different circumstances, and be better prepared for life in this increasingly fast-changing world.

If you are able *to give and to commit*, your experiences and relationships will be enriched. The more you put into something, the more you will get out of it. People who cannot commit and who keep themselves on the outside may feel 'safe' from disappointments or having to expose themselves, but they will remain isolated and will have a poorer life for it.

If you have sound *common sense*, you have an inner 'library' of views and practical experiences which offer you generalised guidance in any situation you may come across. It provides a sense of direction and a feeling of security, knowing that your overall 'view of the world' will guide you when there is no one else to consult.

How do you get good self-esteem?

Self-esteem comes from others:

- valuing you
- approving of you
- spending time with you
- understanding you
- trusting you
- respecting you
- being committed to you
- being 'on your side'

The only way infants or young children can discover themselves and believe that they are likeable and lovable is through having someone else responding to them; liking and loving them and understanding their needs and feelings. That someone else has to be the key and regular carer, who is invariably the mother. This is the bottom line. They believe in themselves if, and only if, others have given them reason to believe that they are worth caring for, are good to be with and are worth sticking up for: if someone else has been committed to them and been seen to be on their side. Robust, permanent or 'core' self-esteem can only be developed if those on whom they rely and whom they trust and adore *demonstrate clearly* to them *and in their own terms* that they are esteemed.

Very young children have to interpret their world through their parents and significant carers. How they are treated and how they *feel* they are treated are potent ingredients in the process of developing their identity. Through offering structure, parents create order out of what can be a terrifying chaos. Through order, infants can learn to predict. Through having their needs acknowledged and met, infants learn that they and their judgements can be trusted, and they learn to trust in return. It is not enough for a parent to say, 'But I love them. Surely they realise that?' We have to break down into separate activities all the ways in which children interpret love.

Children receive messages from us all the time. Inevitably these are both good and bad. We cannot say the right things all the time. We will be more or less tolerant, kind or thoughtful depending upon our state of mind. This begins to matter only when the negative and 'put-down' messages significantly outweigh the supportive and understanding ones. Later, when the child begins to socialise and spend time with a wider circle of people, the messages can be received from a variety of sources. They will still rely on you for their core self-image, but it will be reinforced, refined or even revised through their relationships with others.

Can a poor self-image gained in the early years be overturned later? If you have spent most of your early years getting bad messages about yourself, and then others outside the family begin to tell you something different because they have found things they like about you, what will be the effect? At first, you won't believe it. This negative reaction is likely to go on for some time. How can you overturn your perception of yourself with just a few instances of 'flattery', for that is how it will be perceived. When it has been said often enough (and it *will* have to be said often), you will begin to rate yourself more highly. For the first time, you will have experienced the intoxicating pleasure of feeling good about yourself. But research shows that this kind of positive affirmation has to be given often for the recipient to remain convinced.

Getting started

How can you help your children to develop a clear and positive self-image? A good starting point is to identify what makes each of your children unique – what makes them who they are.

Step One

Write down what you think their personality is – strengths and weaknesses. Include those bits you would prefer not to be there. If you are feeling particularly negative about them, get someone else who knows them well to sit down with you and make you realise they have good features too.

For example, your child:

> adapts easily to new situations
> cares deeply about things
> is quick to cry
> finds it hard to concentrate
> finds it hard to share things
> likes to be involved in 'real' jobs
> lives in a fantasy world
> is very resilient
> is generous
> likes quiet time
> does not like to be interrupted
> likes playing with younger children
> finds it hard to tell the truth
> is tidy/untidy

Step Two

See if you can find any connection between the characteristics that you like and those that you do not care for so much. They may be two sides of the same coin.

For example, you may like the way they are quick to make choices, take decisions and seem to know their mind, but not like the way they constantly argue about doing things their way. But isn't this part of the same thing? You may like the way they can stand up for themselves when playing with their friends, but not like it when they are assertive with you. Again, isn't this the same strength coming out in a different place? Think positive!

Step Three

Write down their likes and dislikes: things that they like to do, things they like to or won't eat, their favourite clothes, and how they like to spend their time. This will add another dimension to your understanding of who they are. If you can identify lots of things they don't like, and very few things they do like, it is time to take improving their self-esteem very seriously. Children who do not have a clear idea of themselves will find it much easier to 'define themselves by the negative'. In other words, to establish their difference, they will say they are *not* like someone else, particularly their siblings. By a process of deduction, they will end up with some kind of picture of themselves. But it is far healthier if someone can say straight away: 'I am this sort of a person', rather than slice away at what they are *not* and see what is left.

Step Four

Think how you can give them space to be themselves, to do the things that they like to do.

For example, if they enjoy having time on their own, have you kept their brothers and sisters out of their hair? Have you taught the others to respect that wish to be undisturbed? If they like playing their favourite game with you, have you made yourself available to do it? If they like football or swimming, do you make sure they get the chance to do them?

Step Five

Tell them from time to time what it is you like about them, and do not just say that it is because they have been 'good'. Spell it out for them so that they realise you understand them and they get a clearer picture of who they are. Help them to feel proud of themselves.

Some further suggestions once you are under way

Value them

Let them know that you realise they are good at certain things and ask for their help using these skills wherever appropriate: *'You are good with your hands. Could you help me mend this?'* You can show them that you enjoy being with them. *'I enjoyed our trip to the shops together.'* Above all, listen to them properly when they want to tell you something.

Approve of and praise them

Say that you like their ideas: *'That was a good idea of something to do.' 'I wouldn't have thought of doing it that way. That was inventive'*; and show that you like their choice of friends: *'Tracey's a good friend; let's have her round again soon.'* Show that you like how they choose to dress: *'That jumper*

looks good with those trousers. You chose well this morning.' Tell them, too, when you think they have done something well. It means more to a child if you praise them for a specific achievement than offering blanket praise.

For example, *'It was a lovely surprise for me that you laid the table/cleared away the toys'* or *'Thanks for letting me know in good time about going out before supper tonight'* both say much more than, *'You are a good girl/boy.'* Reward them with praise and your attention rather than with presents, unless the presents come as an unusual surprise. Material rewards can too easily become something the child negotiates and manipulates.

Spend time with them
Children value you spending time alone with them, both on their terms – doing what they want to do – and on yours. *'It's half an hour until tea. What would you like us to play?'* Or alternatively, *'Come and talk to me while I/help me to sort out this cupboard.'*

Show you understand them
Try to imagine how they will be feeling about something and voice it by telling them how you think it might be for them: *'It must have been really embarrassing for you to have left your dinner money at home again.'* *'I know you don't enjoy tidying your room but you can't see where to tread safely.'* Think carefully before treating every child in the family the same. Although it is important to be seen to be fair in your overall handling, identical treatment can ignore their separate identities, personalities and differing needs.

Trust them

Give them age-appropriate responsibilities and assume that they will carry them out; for example, brushing their teeth, putting used clothes in the linen basket, getting themselves dressed in the morning. This will also develop a wider sense of responsibility and will encourage independence. If they feel strongly about something, trust them to know themselves and let them influence what happens to them in relation to such things as friendships, how much they want to eat, how warm or cold they are feeling. Assume they know the rules and your expectations. If you say, 'Don't forget to . . .' or 'You *will* remember to . . .' you are actually suggesting that they cannot be trusted, which may result in a defiant challenge rather than compliance. Assume that they will be able to be independent from you, but be accessible if they need you; and don't hover over them when they are trying to do something new, or help them with it – unless they ask you to.

Respect them

Be willing to compromise, for children sometimes have valid reasons for disagreeing. You do not undermine your authority by sometimes letting them 'win'; in fact, you increase your authority. (See 'Compromise', Chapter Five.) Listen to them; give them choices to allow some self-determination and autonomy; be seen to be fair and apologise to them if you know you have been unreasonable.

Show your commitment to them

Spend time with them; play with them; talk to them; support them, at school and in things they like to do; and be there for them.

Be on their side

Be their last point of refuge in distress, their safety net, somewhere to hide and, when they need it, act as a supportive friend who sees their point of view. And doing at least one thing from each of the above categories will reinforce their certainty that you are their ally, not their enemy.

What two ideas can you think of . . . ?
-
-

(For more on praise, trust, time, etc., see Chapter Five.)

What else can you do? The idea of 'the balanced activity diet'

These days, parents are only too familiar with health experts telling them to feed their children properly. We are told that by the age of eight children are already affecting their adult life expectancy by what they eat and how much exercise they take. We are being persuaded to reduce the dependence on sugar and fat and instead give them a more balanced diet to include vegetables, fruit, carbohydrate and protein.

In the same way, we should look at how our children spend their time. The greater the variety of things they do and enjoy doing, the better will they know themselves, discover talents and be able to use their time as adults, and the more well-rounded and fulfilled they will be.

The balanced activity diet can have a profound and

important impact on self-esteem as well. The more spheres the child can try, the more she is likely not only to find something which she can be good at to make her feel proud, but also to have the chance to be herself, to try out herself, in many different ways. For example, a child who watches television all the time is likely to have very little idea about the full range of her capabilities. A child gifted at playing the piano, and who does little else, will have little idea about her other talents or interests. If at any stage she decides to stop playing, she could be left with a very uncomfortable void. The child who is fanatical about sports but later receives a permanent injury preventing him from doing anything could similarly be left feeling empty. It is just as true, then, with pastimes which are generally approved of, as with those like watching television or playing computer games, which are sometimes frowned upon: a single interest which crowds out others encourages the child to begin to rely on that for their sense of security because it is familiar and safe territory. It does nothing to encourage the degree of social flexibility and confidence which can remove the anxiety from new situations – a real advantage in today's changing world. A single interest – or, even worse, inactivity – does not help your child to develop the confidence to take risks, other than, perhaps, the death-defying risks of bravado which children needing instant acclaim and attention from their peers are willing to flaunt.

Bruno Bettelheim warned parents against implementing a contrived 'balanced diet' of activities because it is too controlling and may deny their children time for free play. Free play certainly is absolutely vital for the development of children's self-esteem; but the idea of the balanced diet is still useful and valid if parents make sure that there is some time when children *are* left alone to develop their imaginations, to play freely through their anxieties in the way in which they feel they need to at the time. Denying a child the chance to play has similar effects to not allowing an adult the chance to sleep and dream. Their sense of reality can become distorted. Like night-dreams, day-dreams and fantasy play are fundamental ways of re-establishing emotional equilibrium. (See page 114.)

What does a balanced diet look like?
- *outdoor* things (walks, tree-climbing, visits to the park, i.e., physical things; playing anything outside)
- *creative* things (drawing, painting, modelling, e.g., with Playdoh, sand, water, cooking, gardening, making and hearing music)
- *social* things (visits to friends and relatives – your friends too so they can learn from you how to socialise)
- *imaginative things* (playing indoor 'tents' with blankets, or trains with cardboard boxes, 'let's pretend' games such as doctors or schools)
- *ball* skills and games
- *unstructured* play (let them fiddle around in a seemingly disorganised way with anything or nothing so that their thoughts can wander at will)
- *bookish* things (read to them, look at pictures in books or magazines, library trips. Let them be with you if you are reading or writing so that they have a model to copy)
- *number* things (counting as part of daily life – stairs, spoons to lay on the table, steps to reach the next lamppost, houses to the postbox, etc.)

What are the essential things to avoid if you want your child to have 'good' self-esteem?

Even if you are doing many of the things suggested above, it is still important to be aware of the responses and behaviours we commonly use that damage a child's self-esteem. Knowing the things that undermine children means, first, that they can be avoided and, second, that if we do say or do something hurtful (which we all do from time to time), we recognise it and can make up for it by going out of our way to repair the damage. Children are very sensitive to criticism. They seem to take it much more to heart than praise. It may therefore take two or three 'boosters', or 'puff-ups', to undo the damage of one insult or 'put-down' and to restore 'ego equilibrium'.

So what should be avoided?

Making approval or love conditional on good behaviour

Children need to be loved for who they are, warts and all, not only when they are well behaved – when they are being who *you want them to be*.

Combining and confusing disapproval of things done with disapproval of the person

When they stray outside the boundaries you have set for them, always make it clear that you are complaining about *what they have done*, not *who they are*. '*That was a silly thing to do*', not '*You are so silly*'.

Blaming them for things that go wrong: 'It's your fault.'

Children are easy targets for blame. It is strangely comforting for us to be able to shirk our responsibility for things which go wrong and instead point our finger at the child who happened to be around. While children should, in some situations, be held responsible for their behaviour, much of the time either they are too young to realise what was going to be the result of their mistakes, or they had very little, directly, to do with the complained-of calamity. *'It's your fault. If you hadn't got me angry, I wouldn't have dropped the plate!'* Blame directs responsibility away from the blamer and on to the blamed. Blame creates guilt and shame which, for young children who take any criticism of what they've done as a criticism of who they are, are complex, confusing and restricting emotions.

Putting them down

'Put-downs' take many forms. These are explored and analysed in detail in Chapter Six. They include criticisms, physical rejections, threats, blame, labels such as 'You are useless', lack of trust, and so on. Adults are often completely unaware of the impact of their clumsy words. Children are so keen to have the approval of those they care about that even minor criticisms can be quite hurtful.

Self-esteem: question check-list

The questions listed below are to be used as a guide *either* if you are not sure what to do in a given situation, *or* just to reflect on the day to see if you are still moving in the right direction. If you are not sure what to do at any time, you do not necessarily need to go to books on the subject, or to spend time on the telephone finding out what your friends would do if they were you. The questions can be seen as a kind of yardstick against which you can check your own common-sense ideas and work things out for yourself. If your idea does not get a 'yes' answer to *any* of the questions below, then you should think again. If it does, then it is OK to do it your way.

- Will this make them feel good, or at least not bad, about themselves?
- Have I shown that I have understood their feelings and/or point of view on anything today?
- Have I shown ány interest in, or asked about, anything they have done today?
- Have I listened to them with my whole-hearted attention, at least once?
- Will they think that I am on their side?

In summary

Children can value, esteem and love themselves only if you have convinced them that you have valued, esteemed and loved them first.

SELF-CONFIDENCE

What is self-confidence?

Self-confidence is:
- trusting your ability to form and sustain relationships
- trusting your ability to complete various tasks well
- knowing that others value your abilities
- trusting your ability to manage new situations
- trusting your own judgements and common sense

Self-confidence is close to but clearly different from self-esteem. Self-esteem, it has been stated, relates to a belief in one's intrinsic worth. It involves a view of your inner self as seen by you from the outside. Self-confidence, by contrast, relates to a judgement about your abilities in the wider world. It involves a view of yourself operating in society, as seen by you from the inside. In answer to the question, 'Who trusts me and believes in me?' the answer is a triumphant, 'I trust and believe in myself!' You then expect that others will have a similar confidence in you.

Trust is a key element of self-confidence. The *Oxford English Dictionary* defines confidence as: 'firm trust; assured expectation; boldness'. Nobody can develop self-confidence if they neither trust themselves nor have an 'assured expectation' about the (therefore predictable and trustworthy) behaviour of others. Children who do not have a measure of consistency and predictability in their lives will find it very hard to acquire the necessary trust either in others or in themselves to become self-confident.

On the other hand, if those who are most important to you clearly trust you and provide a consistent environment, you can begin to trust yourself, your judgements and the behaviour and decisions of others around you. This is the beginning of common sense – applying your knowledge of the predictable world around you, knowing something about yourself and how to relate to others. Self-confidence means that you are confident not merely that your parents like, love and want you but that others show interest in, appreciate and want to spend time with you too. It is your wider acceptability, by your peers and others, that is crucial. It is something which therefore develops after infancy, when children begin to socialise outside the familiar environment of their family.

Natural self-confidence comes from within. But self-confidence is also something which people can create, and often do create, on top of doubts about their core self. We can acquire skills and accomplishments. We can learn to entertain and amuse. We can discover techniques to control and to avoid many of life's uncertainties. We can, through later experience and observation, develop and supplement social skills. We all build on and enrich ourselves as we live our lives, gaining knowledge and insights as well as confidence as we mature. This is the joy of living. Teaching our children how to unfold or unwrap themselves to discover new treasures and talents within them, much as they do in the game Pass the Parcel, and to learn to trust themselves and their abilities in new situations is something of great value which will give them life-long benefit.

Why is it important to develop self-confidence?

Self-confidence helps us to be:

- open and outgoing
- straightforward
- trusting
- trustworthy and reliable
- determined and able to stick at things

How do children acquire self-confidence?

Self-confidence comes from:

- being accepted for who you are
- having someone show confidence in you
- knowing there is something you are good at
- having firm expectations of other people's behaviour
- not having too many experiences of failure
- not being afraid of failing

- developing competence with the safety of a parent close by
- seeing others you admire and copy being confident and happy

Getting started

There are three necessary components of self-confidence. If you think that you need to boost your child's self-confidence, you will need to take action to encourage each one. The three components are: Trust and Predictability; Competence; Sociability.

Trust and predictability

Step One

Routines are important for developing feelings of trust and security. Think about the routines and relationships between you, your family and friends and whether they keep to a pattern. Will your child begin each day with a reasonably clear idea of what will happen and when, either in terms of events, or who they will meet? How predictable are the relationships in their lives? Do they see certain people regularly, or do they come and go in an apparently unplanned and arbitrary way? Are the relationships which they have with the adults and children around them ones which they can trust, or do the people involved – including, perhaps, you – 'blow hot and cold on them' in a way which they will see as unexpected? How predictable is *their* behaviour?

Step Two

If you realise that there are aspects of family life that your child will not easily be able to predict relating to work or school collections, review current arrangements and make any possible changes to increase the sense of pattern and 'assured expectation' in their life. If there is not much that is within your control to change, make sure that you explain in advance both *why* things have to happen in the way that they do, and *what* is going to happen on any particular day. Where relevant, try speaking to key people about making either the *frequency* or the *content* of their visits more predictable. This will be especially important if a child sees a parent who no longer lives with them.

Competence (being good at things)

Step One

Under the headings of different skills, list the activities which you think your child is good at and which he likes to do and make him feel good. These skills can be:

practical	e.g., seeing how to make or mend things, and build things
physical	e.g., good at sport (kicking/catching balls, swimming, running, etc.)
mental	e.g., having good ideas about things, being good at solving practical problems, good at school work
social	e.g., good at playing with others; kind and considerate; good at making new friends; sensing when people need to be left alone or quiet
process	e.g., being good at trying new things, sticking at difficult tasks, etc.

Step Two

Ask *them* what they like doing and what they think they are good at. It will be very interesting to learn if these are the same things that you have written down. It is quite likely they will be the same, because children will naturally value themselves for the same things which they have realised you value in them. If there are things which you have listed and they have not, make sure you let them know your feelings about what they are good at. If they have listed things which you have not, ask yourself why. Is it because you have a different set of values? Can you adjust these to accept their view of themselves? If you see these attributes as negative (for example, they might say they are good at fighting), consider whether they are already judging themselves outside your scales because they feel they cannot measure up to your expectations. For interest's sake, try the same exercise with the things they are not so good at.

Step Three

If neither you nor they have been able to find anything that demonstrates competence, offer them chances to try new skills. Everyone needs to feel good at something. Find out from the library, school or local sports centre what children's activities are available in your area.

Sociability

Step One

Trust and develop their social skills. Involve them moderately in your social life. If you have them with you, it shows not only that you are happy to be with them but also that you trust that they will behave sensibly and appropriately.

Getting used to being in new situations and learning to talk with different people will increase their confidence considerably. Keep it in proportion, though. If you do it too much, they might not appreciate your boundaries and learn that you are entitled to your own time, without them. Give them advance warning of your feelings – of bad temper, tiredness, sadness, frustration or whatever. *'I've had a difficult day at work today. I might be snappy. It might be best for you if you steer clear of me for a while.'* Or *'I've had an argument with X today and I'm feeling rather sore. If I rat at you, don't take it seriously.'* This not only teaches them techniques for managing their own feelings, but also gives them a chance to learn sensitivity to the feelings and moods of others, and to accommodate and adjust as appropriate. These are essential social skills, immensely valuable for later life, and even for their lives at home or at school here and now.

Step Two
Encourage them to play, with you and others in the family, and with friends. Restrict the use of pastimes, for example television and computer games, that do not necessarily involve talking, sharing and compromise, i.e., social interaction.

Some further suggestions once you are under way

Trust and predictability
Chart all changes. Give as much advance warning of changes as possible.

If possible, introduce big changes little by little, so change is not an uncomfortable and frightening experience. Introduce changes one at a time; for example, don't ask your child to cope with starting school and you going back to work, or changing your work routines, at the same time.

Make sure that the 'do's and don'ts' family rules are enforced consistently. If they are not, maybe you have too many. Write down which ones are most important to you, ensure everyone is clear what you expect of them, and then make sure that they comply! If you don't think you have any rules, and life can get chaotic at times, then make some. All children need boundaries; that is, limits beyond which they know they should not go.

What two ideas can you think of . . .?
-
-

Competence

Ask for their help with something they are good at to show that you appreciate their skill. For example, if they are good at thinking things out, you can ask them to help you with a decision you have to make. If they are practical, invite them to help you mend something. If they are strong and well co-ordinated, ask them to help you lift or move things.

Acknowledge their pride in their achievements. Wherever you can, reinforce their own good feelings about themselves. *'You must have felt really proud when you managed to do that.' 'I bet that made you feel good!'*

When they are trying something new, let them know that you believe they can do it. Let them see that you have confidence in them.

> What two ideas can you think of . . . ?
> •
> •

Sociability

Encourage them to experience plenty of different social situations, though at the beginning in the safety of your company. At first, let them sit and watch you as you mix with friends. Make sure you take a toy or something else for them to play with while you talk.

If you do not have a wide circle of friends, see if you can take them to places where there are other children, for example a playgroup or the playground. Perhaps you could suggest getting together with a neighbour for a cup of tea, or go and visit someone in your family. Local libraries and family centres often run story times in the afternoon for under-fives. They will also have information about other activities in the area for small children and for parents feeling alone.

> What two ideas can you think of . . .?
> •
> •

What are the important things to avoid?

- Do not undermine their feelings about their own ability.
- Do not burst their bubble of confidence if they believe they can do something.

- Do not constantly tell them that other children, or you, can do whatever they have done better.
- Do not confuse being confident in their ability to manage without you with abdicating responsibility.
- Do not question their ability to be a good friend to others or, indeed, to themselves.

Self-confidence: question check-list

As with self-esteem, the questions listed below are to be used as a guide *either* if you are not sure what to do in a given situation, or just to reflect on the day to see if you are offering enough scope for the development of confidence.

- Have I given them the chance to do something they are good at?
- Have I valued anything that they think they have done well?
- Have I acknowledged their feelings of achievement (even if I think they could have done better)?
- Have I given them a chance to socialise in a variety of different situations, with both their own friends and mine?
- Have I demonstrated my confidence in their ability to cope with and function in the world out there by taking them with me when I go out?
- When they had to do something new for the first time, did I offer them the security of being close by? Did I acknowledge their worries about it, and did I show confidence in their ability to cope? Did I praise them afterwards for having managed the situation well?

- How predictable and structured is their life at the moment? Have I kept them properly informed of and explained any changes and upsets?
- Can I introduce any routines which will create a greater sense of pattern, consistency and security to their lives?

In summary

Children will develop self-confidence only if you have first shown trust and confidence in them and have provided an environment within which they can predict and trust.

SELF-RELIANCE

What is self-reliance?

Self-reliance is the ability to cope on your own: to know how to manage time and to function and think independently, combined with the ability to negotiate risks and solve problems. With self-reliance, there is no need for other people's approval before moving forward or doing something new. There is no need, either, for detailed and constant guidance on how to achieve the end product. You can rely on yourself. Self-reliance is about tasks and skills – knowing how to do things, how to achieve things, or how to manage things; but it also indicates the ability both to be alone and to think things through on your own.

Self-reliance is broader than self-confidence. Self-confidence relates to what we can do, to specific skills and aptitudes. Self-reliance is about being *independent*, *creative* and *self-sufficient*; having confidence, if you like, in our inner resources to enable us as individuals to adapt and manage on our own.

Why is it important to develop self-reliance?

Self-reliance helps us to be:
- active
- independent
- creative
- competent
- spontaneous

It enables children to be confident in their own ideas and carry things through to completion, so it helps if they have sufficient strength or co-ordination to prevent the lack of either from obstructing achievement. Self-reliant people can set their own goals, know that help is available if it is needed and are not put off by setbacks.

Management trainers often describe the world as being divided into three types of people: those who make things happen; those who watch things happening; and those who notice nothing until after and then ask, 'What's happened?' Those who have good self-reliance (and confidence and self-esteem) are the people who make things happen.

We do not need to think of our children doing this on a grand scale: becoming a captain of industry, a Nobel scientist or literary genius. The objective need not be to make a difference to *others*; simply to have the skills to retain better control of *their* lives and keep open choices for *them* to enhance the quality of those lives. And in any fast-changing society, the successful individuals are those who can both cope with change and contribute to it; in other words, those who can show flexibility, initiative and creativity.

Self-reliant at what?

We can encourage self-reliance from quite an early age, within our own homes. As soon as children show that they can manage things for themselves, however slowly, clumsily or imperfectly, we should give them opportunities to do so, gradually as children become more competent and responsible. Very young children have a virtually unstoppable drive to become independent. Before they are confronted with adult concepts of failure, they are willing to try and try again until they master the task in view. They desperately want to lose their dependency and become free, like adults or older siblings, to do things on their own and they often reject a parent's help with astonishing passion! If we prevent them from trying and instead do things for them, or transmit frustration or disapproval when they do not quite do it right, we will damage their growing belief in themselves and stunt their ability to make judgements and decisions. We turn them into automatons who can only act when instructed. The stages of developing self-reliance will look something like this:

First Stage

Managing their own life and person: e.g., feeding, toileting, washing, cleaning teeth, getting dressed. As soon as babies are able to get some food into their mouths by their own hands, they should be encouraged to do it. As soon as they are able to tell, most of the time, when they need a wee, we should give them the responsibility to manage this. If we keep overall control at this stage, we will be saying that they cannot be trusted. By the time children start school, they should be wiping their own bottoms and dressing themselves.

Second Stage
Carrying out their own ideas and directing their own play.

Third Stage
Managing things within the home and taking responsibility for some domestic chores (for example, keeping their rooms tidy, putting their used clothes in the linen basket, laying the table); organising how they occupy and entertain themselves within agreed guidelines; managing their own pocket money. By this time, children should be allowed to be involved in the decisions which affect their lives, for example, spending pocket money how they wish, which after-school activities they take up, agreeing contracts specifying rewards granted for extra responsibilities and commitments.

Fourth Stage
Managing themselves outside the home, e.g., school, homework, getting their things ready, their social life, out-of-school clubs and activities, music lessons, etc.

Fifth Stage
Managing others within and outside the home, e.g., baby-sitting.

Letting Go

Clearly, you cannot encourage self-reliance in your children if you are not prepared to stand back and, progressively, let go. Doing that in the right amounts and at the right time, is very hard to judge. How much responsibility and independence you give should, of necessity, depend on the age and personality of each child and on your own circumstances. Giving them too much of either before they are emotionally or developmentally ready for it can be as damaging as not giving them enough.

Letting go too late. Some parents wait on their offspring hand and foot to prove their devotion, seeing this as an essential constituent of good parenting. But what they are really proving is their need to feel needed and to be in control, not their devotion. They are hooking their children like a fisherman, keeping a line out on them and winding them in from time to time, jerking them to the bank, just to prove that they are still in charge.

Letting go too soon. If children get too much independence too soon when they still need support and attention, they will feel abandoned and shamed, not independent and proud.

How do children become self-reliant?

Self-reliance comes through having:
- responsibility
- independence and autonomy
- relevant practical experience and common sense
- scope for self-determination
- problem-solving skills
- good fitness and health

Responsibility

Responsibility means having the job of carrying something out, and being held accountable for it. This differs from independence, which involves taking decisions about how, where and when a task should be completed. Children should experience appropriate and increasing responsibility as they mature. Once you can take care of yourself, you become able to take care of others and have others rely on you. So children should be given responsibility for themselves in the first instance.

Later, they should be expected to take some reasonable and progressive responsibility for others. This transfer is important, though the qualification 'reasonable' can be critical; for example, you might consider leaving your twelve-year-old to look after a two-year-old sibling for half an hour, but to leave them together for a whole day would not be appropriate. It would be asking too much. To have others rely on you to do something encourages 'task commitment', because there is outside pressure to carry something through. Children who are given reasonable responsibility feel trusted, competent and respected and find out more about what they can do.

Independence and autonomy

Self-reliance and independence are mutually reinforcing. The more self-reliant you are, the more you can manage independence. The more you experience independence, the more you build up the confidence and skills to develop self-reliance. Independence is having the opportunity to take decisions and look after oneself free from direction. If children are encouraged to problem-solve and experiment with different approaches on their own at home, they'll have a head start when they reach school. Parents must provide the opportunities, and time, to allow children to achieve practical tasks; they must be tolerant of the methods needed to achieve them; and they must know how to deal with the inevitable frustration.

'Independence without abandonment': getting the balance right

However, independence must not be foisted on children too early regardless of appropriateness merely because it is convenient for the parent. Sometimes, a family's practical needs are the trigger for increasing independence and it is appropriate. But it is nonetheless important to review the relevance of any motives and to be sensitive to a child's perception of these. An *apparent* ability to cope with the extra demands might also conceal a continuing need for company, guidance and attention. The right balance to aim for is 'independence without abandonment'.

If a child feels 'put upon', 'used' or abandoned as a result of the greater responsibility and independence given to him, his self-reliance and self-esteem could be damaged, not enhanced. The independence will be counterproductive, and will cause him anguish and self-doubt that will impede self-expression and confidence.

Relevant practical experience and common sense

Common sense develops through having relevant and practical experiences. Someone who is self-reliant should know, amongst other things, how to:

- feed themselves and, preferably, cook
- take sensible decisions about spending money within a budget
- manage public transport and crossing roads

- use the computer to get information
- react appropriately in various emergency situations

Problem-solving skills

With appropriate support and guidance, children should be encouraged to solve their own practical and relationship problems. For example, if we are asked the common question 'What can I do, I'm bored?', instead of phoning a friend to come over every time, or playing a game with them, you can help them to write a list of things which they like to do and play – on their own or with others – (simply illustrated if they cannot read) so they can look at it in future to get ideas and take the decision themselves.

Physical fitness

To be self-reliant, we also need a certain degree of strength and physical competence, and this is as true for women and girls as it is for men and boys. Sport and physical activity are important in establishing or improving good coordination and fitness. Exercise provides us with longer-term benefits, and is good for our health, stamina, motivation, general well-being and energy levels. If it is so beneficial for adults, and if an active childhood improves later health, we should make doubly sure that our children are keeping exercised and fit.

Unfortunately, research shows that children today are getting far less exercise than they used to. In fact, some people take more notice of their dog's need for exercise than their children's. If we have a dog, we make sure it has a walk twice a day. For many of our children, their only exercise is PE once a week at school and little else, being driven to most places, playing more indoors and generally leading a much more sedentary life.

Balancing security and independence

Independence is a vital and exciting part of growing up. Developing a pride in your competence; experiencing challenges and surviving; experimenting with risks and different ways of doing things; gaining more control over what happens to you and learning to set your own boundaries; these are all essential if a child is to become an autonomous and responsible adult. It is vital that children have new freedoms and responsibilities, *as* and *when* they are ready to cope with them.

Unfortunately, the world outside the home is becoming an increasingly dangerous place. Parents are naturally worried about giving children greater freedom to play and travel without adult supervision. Instead of encouraging children to go off on their own and experiment, giving out rope gradually, they supervise, chaperone, constrain and contain them. Fear of traffic accidents and molestation means children get driven or walked to school and friends' homes. They are discouraged from playing even in the front garden let alone the street or the park. Having children safely indoors, of course, frees parents from worry and gives them a wonderful feeling of relief. To add virtue to self-interest, they kid themselves that what they are doing is in the best interest of their child. But is it? Is it possible that we are losing a proper sense of balance on the issue of security versus independence? Fearful messages about attacks by strangers could be damaging children's willingness and ability to 'go' even where the parents are happy to 'let go'.

Children and young people are now getting very mixed messages about how capable they are or ought to be. We have almost got the issue upside down. When children are small, we give them too much independence; too many choices about things which give them an inappropriate degree of responsibility and control. It gives them too much power before they are ready to manage it and when parents still need to be in charge and taking responsibility. When children enter their pre-teens, however, when they need to feel confident and be wresting some of those controls into their own hands, we tell them that it is a fearful world and, in effect, they cannot be trusted to manage themselves and cope.

The best way to acquire coping skills is through experience. Experience also builds common sense and lessens fear. If we were to drive less and walk or use public transport more, over time children would develop road sense and a rational attitude to traffic. If we were to walk and be out and about more, children would develop a better sense of what is normal or strange behaviour, and be more confident about reacting in a sensible way. Confronting fears keeps them in proportion. Hiding from them makes them grow. Staying in cars or indoors is no way to acquire life skills.

The problem goes further than these practical issues. Susan Kegerreis, in a paper entitled 'Independent mobility and children's mental and emotional development' (*Children, Transport and the Quality of Life*, ed. M. Hillman), argues that:

> *being able to go places on their own is extremely important in fostering children's development . . . Opportunities to be on our own are opportunities to*

practise, to try ourselves out . . . If we do not have such
opportunities, our identity is harder to establish, self-
esteem harder to build up and social adjustment –
finding out how to operate in and belong to a wider
society – harder to achieve.

The two main culprits are, then, the car and crime, but
they are not the only things which are reducing the
amount children go out on their own. The demise of the
corner shop means that fewer children 'nip out' to buy
groceries. Public transport is less available. With more
school mergers and greater use of private schooling,
children have to travel further to school. The increasing
popularity of home-based entertainment, such as multi-
channel television, DVDs and computer-based games,
means that children are less likely to go out or make their
own creative entertainment.

Balancing rights and responsibilities

Self-reliance is about gaining independence and rights at
the same time as taking on new responsibilities. If children
have more responsibilities, they should also have more
rights to go with them, so they can see that it is part of
growing up and they are proud about it happening. If they
get more rights as they get older, they should also get more
responsibilities to balance out, to avoid them becoming
entirely self-centred. When coupled with extra rights, and
when increased at the same time as birthdays or other
events acknowledging increasing maturity, responsibilities
are not resented. Indeed, quite the opposite; they are
accepted with pride.

Getting started – real-world tasks:

Step One

Make a list of anything you think you can give them responsibility for, e.g., brushing their teeth, getting dressed, fetching the evening paper, feeding the cat/dog, laying the table, tidying their toys, or whatever task is appropriate for their age. If they are near a birthday, give them the responsibility from that date, with due preparation, so they feel a sense of pride in having the responsibility and it is seen as a natural part of growing up, not an unwelcome chore foisted upon them.

Step Two

Balance the new responsibilities with rights.

Step Three

Trust them. Give them the space to do the task in and the space to make mistakes. Walk away.

Step Four

Let go. Gradually withdraw to increase their independence. Let them take increasing control of themselves and be involved in agreeing the new boundaries to that independence. It is essential to encourage and approve of developments towards independence, to convey the message that you trust them to be able to manage and that you approve of their lessening need for you.

Some further suggestions once you are under way

- Involve them in real-world tasks such as cooking, gardening, mending things, decorating, changing plugs.

- Encourage physical activity to build up strength, coordination, morale and confidence.
- Offer limited and achievable goals that allow children to progress step by step.
- Always reward (verbal praise is usually sufficient) even minimal achievement.
- Let them achieve the task their way.
- If they express an urge to do something, respond to their spontaneity and confidence and try to let it happen, as soon as possible. Let them prove it to themselves.
- Let them define their own challenges, not adopt yours.
- Manage the mess. Your fear of 'mess' should not impede a child's need to create and experiment. Have clear rules about such things as putting down protective newspaper or plastic sheets, wearing aprons, doing certain things outdoors, the use of felt pens or other materials that might stain.
- Let them play alone sometimes to encourage their imagination and to demonstrate that they *can* entertain themselves in fulfilling ways.
- If they have done something which pleases them and which they are proud of, that is good enough. *It does not matter what other people think* (unless it is school and it is something for them to evaluate).
- Warn of the potential for disappointment if their goals are unrealistic.

What are the important things to avoid?

- Never say that they are stupid if they haven't managed something.

- Don't have too high expectations.
- Don't make approval conditional on success. Trying hard, or even just having a go, is just as important.
- Don't hover over them while they are doing it. Your presence is quite likely to put them off. To walk away and leave them to it is a statement of trust, and demonstrates an assumption that it will happen.
- Beware of completing a task for them before they are finished. (Sometimes this is a practical necessity but, wherever possible, don't.) Bite back your frustration and do not convey your disappointment if they have not managed it.

Self-reliance: question check-list

- Have I given them the chance to do some real task by themselves today?
- Have I noticed, acknowledged and shown approval for any instances of independence, or have I stamped on them because for them to do it causes me inconvenience?
- When they last had an idea about doing something which needed assistance, did I help it happen either then or later, or let it fall through a crack?

Conclusion

Children can become self-reliant only if you have encouraged their independence; given them practice in taking decisions which concern themselves; and have shown them, first, that they can be relied upon.

3

Building a Firm Foundation:

II THE REPAIR KIT

Almost all relationships have times when they reach rock-bottom. This includes the relationship between parent and child. At these times, which may be short-lived or be much longer-lasting, you may become not only depressed but also fearful either that your child will be a life-long loser, or that you cannot be an adequate parent: even, sometimes, that you are not the right person to bring up your child. Mutual trust will be low. Self-respect will be low. Patterns of behaviour and response can get established, set in motion by either of you, which make you feel that you can do nothing right. Your child's behaviour, and your responses to her at these times, is so awful that you are too embarrassed to discuss it with any of your friends. There may even be knock-on effects in her behaviour at school which you are called in to talk about. Blame and guilt will be there in quantity. The scenes which you experience within your four walls do not appear in any of the standard child-rearing textbooks, so you cannot even try to work out in the privacy of your home what has gone wrong and what to do about it.

Why do relationships sometimes get like this, and what tools do you need to repair the damage?

Bad times can happen for a wide variety of reasons. They rarely happen for no reason, because (as some might be tempted to think) a child has suddenly turned into a 'bad apple'. It may be that the *child* is having to cope with a stressful new experience such as the arrival of a new baby in the family, starting school, separation from someone close, or with a parent starting or changing jobs. It may be that either or both of the *parents* are having problems in their lives – for example debt, marital difficulties, the threat or reality of redundancy, or the death of someone close to them. Each of these events involves change and uncertainty. And uncertainty breeds insecurity.

If anyone within a family, parent or child, feels insecure, they will respond to things very differently: usually less consistently and less appropriately. Moods make people unpredictable. Children very quickly detect changed moods, or if a parent's mind is preoccupied with something else. They do not like things to feel different. They will seek reassurance through getting your attention and confirmation of your continuing love for them. If, after trying several times, they do not get it, they will try to protect themselves both from fear of the unfamiliar and from the pain of apparent rejection.

They protect themselves by telling themselves that they neither value their parents nor need to have their approval through trying to be cooperative or 'good', because it hurts too much when they want it and do not get it. They may even take this one step further and try to take control of events and their life by becoming uncontrollable. It will not make them happy. But at least they will not feel at the mercy of people and events which they cannot predict or understand. The problem, then, may go deeper than poor discipline. But children's response to insecurity, stress, anxiety or unhappiness frequently takes the form of challenge and disobedience. Repairing the relationship will often require a two-pronged approach dealing with both the *symptom*: poor discipline; and the *cause*: insecurity.

POWER PLAY: UNDERSTANDING THE BEHAVIOUR WHEN THERE IS BREAKDOWN

It may be helpful to understand and accept two things when you sit down to straighten matters out. These are very important.

- When your child's behaviour is awful, try not to take it personally. Remember that she is doing it primarily to protect herself and to get attention, and because she is angry. She will not be doing it to 'get at' you. You should not need to retaliate.
- Through taking on the responsibility for putting a stop to the downward spiral, you will be able to re-establish your authority. Both parents and children feel very threatened by the loss of parental authority. The reality is that children do not want to be in control. They want, and need, the parent clearly to be in charge.

POWER, AUTHORITY AND POOR BEHAVIOUR

These difficult times are usually characterised by poor behaviour, ill-discipline and a total disregard for the house rules and the needs of others. If you feel that your child is out of your control and winding you up outrageously, the chances are that, out of desperation, you will decide that you need to reassert control. Probably without much warning you will seize the remaining power you have and start laying down the law, introducing strong punishments, or issuing threats and bribes – in other words, getting your way however you have to do it. But demonstrations of power usually produce power responses and, far from giving you good feelings of being back in the driving seat, you can end up feeling less in control than when you started. Reversing the downward spiral when both parent and child are using various power tactics is important, necessary and not always easy. It will almost certainly require a triple strategy:

- action to draw and enforce clear boundaries to reintroduce security
- action to improve your confidence and self-esteem
- action to improve your child's confidence and self-esteem

Understanding how parents and children both use and respond to power is an important part of the unwinding process.

Power and authority: what is the difference?

Power and authority are closely related, but they are different. That difference is important. For too long the two notions have been bundled together in parenting attitudes. The result has been that either parents feel it is within their 'rights' to use both, and the child can end up terrorised; or they reject both, leaving the child to flounder in an authority vacuum, not receiving either direction or guidance. What is the difference between power and authority? Why is it good for parents to exploit their natural *authority*, as parents, but not desirable for them to depend on using their *power*?

Authority is, of course, a form of power. It is usually understood to mean 'legitimate' power, or 'accepted' power. Power can be 'accepted' in two senses. Firstly, in relation to *the person who has power*. Is it right that a particular person has power – the ability to control the behaviour of others – in a particular circumstance? Democratically elected political leaders have power; we accept that. Having won elections, they have a right to make decisions – sometimes ones we do not like – on our behalf. Secondly, in relation to *how they use that power*. Do they use their power in a way which most people would agree was acceptable? For example, most people in democracies would agree that it is acceptable for politicians to take decisions about taxes, but not ones which concern what colour car we drive, or whether we can travel outside our country.

There are several circumstances in which people broadly agree that it is acceptable for someone to have both authority and the implied access to the means to enforce that authority (the tools of power) if that is the only way to exercise it. One situation, just mentioned, is where people have been *elected* to the position of authority – *political* authority. Another is where someone *traditionally* and *legally* has authority in that role, such as a parent or a teacher. A third is where someone seems to command authority because of their personality, and naturally takes control when it is helpful for someone to take either the lead or the responsibility.

Parental authority

This book is concerned, of course, with parental authority. But looking at other examples can help to illustrate the difference between power and authority. Authority, then, does not always involve taking decisions about how others should behave in the sense of purely exercising control over them. It is also about taking the lead, offering guidance and, above all, accepting responsibility. People in authority take responsibility for others. They have to be sensitive to the needs of the whole community they manage, and operate in a way which delivers the greatest good to the greatest number. They cannot give in to one group exclusively at the expense of another. This is very similar to the role which should be taken by the parent within the family.

Ideally, if someone has authority, or is in a position of authority, there should be little need to enforce the authority using the tools of power which are available. But we do not live in an ideal world. Children do challenge, will challenge, and even need to challenge. It is a very rare child, and a not very well-rounded one, who does everything she is told. So there will often be times when we will have to back up our authority and enforce our decisions. In other words, we resort to power when our authority does not 'work', and use techniques other than merely asking to make people do what we want. These techniques can be called *the tools of power*. Provided the techniques we use are both fair and reasonable, and keep within the boundaries of what would be considered 'acceptable' – which means, broadly, that they meet the requirement that 'the punishment fits the crime' and are not designed to humiliate – we will not be either abusing our power or using illegitimate power. But resorting to power too often, even if it is not over-strict, can cause resentment and can lead to the disintegration of the relationship. First, we will look in more detail at the tools of power which both parents and children have at their disposal. Second, ways to re-establish and support parental authority will be considered.

How parents use power

Parents have both power and authority. Of course they have power: they are physically stronger; they are better at using words to get their way; for a significant number of years they control the child's access to money, food, mobility, entertainment and independence, things which children either need or desire; and, psychologically, most parents will need the child less than the child needs the parents. It is a profoundly unequal relationship and the scope for abuse is vast.

Many of the problems which parents have in keeping an organised and calm home stem, as has already been mentioned, from people believing that power and authority are the same thing. 'Liberal' or 'permissive' parents who reject the available tools of parental power can end up throwing out their authority at the same time. In striving to be 'equal', they can fail to give the vital lead which every child needs, and fail to take the responsibility for their child as she grows up. At the other end of the spectrum, 'authoritarian' parents, who feel that they must always be 'in authority' and in command, can believe that it is quite acceptable regularly to use the tools of power to maintain and reinforce this position.

The tools of power

Power is a reality of life. It is a feature, hidden or otherwise, of most relationships. Power does not only involve physical force. People also use emotional and verbal techniques to get their way. Parents may believe that because they do not hit or physically damage their children they are not using power. They would be mistaken. Children are sensitive to all the tools of power used by adults.

The tools of power used by parents include:

Physical	• hitting
	• hurting
	• damaging belongings
Verbal	• bribery
	• ridicule
	• threats
	• sarcasm
	• shouting
Emotional	• withdrawal
	• withholding food, liberty, etc.

How children use power

Despite their physical inferiority, children very quickly learn to identify the tools of power available to them. Power is not just about having control. It is also being able to *take* control when you want to. Children have many devices at their disposal to take control.

Defensive or attention-seeking behaviour takes the form of:

- disruption: breaking the flow, the silence
- challenge: testing the boundaries and your reactions

- crying/whingeing/whining/moaning
- refusing to acknowledge you or what you say
- damaging your property, or a sibling's toys
- damaging things in their bedroom
- walking out of the house
- refusing to talk or answer questions, particularly when cornered
- being verbally and physically abusive to you or to other family members
- food or clothes fads

These tools of power are used when parent and child are desperate. They are the responses of someone trying to keep one step ahead; trying to pay the other back for the last challenge or humiliation, tit-for-tat style. They are not usually rational. They are almost always inappropriate and unreasonable.

They are inappropriate for two reasons. First, because they escalate quickly and soon lose any relationship to the scale of the issue at hand. We can find ourselves saying and doing the most outrageous things when the initial fight was over something quite petty. Second, and far more important, because they do not work. *They solve nothing*. When the fight spirals out of control, then is the time to take stock and agree a plan of action.

Getting started

Step One
Repair your own self-esteem. Do something that you enjoy doing, that you are good at, something which you used to take pride in being good at (see Chapter Four).

Step Two

Make the first move and take responsibility. Don't wait for the child to make it better. She is only a child. You are the adult and you must take the responsibility for bringing about change. Take the responsibility for the state of the relationship away from her. She will not understand why the relationship has changed and become difficult and will almost certainly be feeling some guilt. Be open about the difficult time you are both having, and avoid blaming and thus stereotyping her and creating the self-fulfilling prophecy. Instead, you can say something like, *'I know that you haven't been yourself lately. I have been pretty horrible too.'* She will not have been feeling happy or proud about how she has been behaving.

Step Three

Make the second, third and fourth moves. Don't expect a quick change or immediate reciprocation from her. Don't make your next moves dependent on her responding with better behaviour straight away. After a bad patch, trust is thin. You have to keep it going. Try to keep cool, not to lose your temper and shout.

Step Four

Rebuild the structure and routines of your family which are likely to have been destroyed by challenges and ill-discipline. Set out clear rules and clear routines, to reintroduce security and predictability. Announce the new rules clearly, and do not debate them. Explain them, and make sure they are not presented as a form of punishment. Choose one or two things to implement and enforce at the beginning – select, perhaps, one time of day and get the new patterns established there before going on to regulate other times. Alternatively, start with the time of day which gets you down most – bedtime or getting ready for school. Keep it simple and manageable. Make sure that your rules are clear and fair, simple to understand and implement, and reasonable. And keep critical comments on her behaviour in other areas to a minimum.

Step Five

Praise her and her good behaviour as much as you can, while you are working on getting her to keep to these new rules, to make her feel loved, lovable and wanted. For some reason we find it much easier to be negative than positive. Provided you are honest about the bad or disruptive things she does, you cannot praise too much. At the same time, try as hard as you can to ignore minor incidents of bad behaviour. Frequent nagging and telling off will only send messages of failure and disapproval. She may then lose the urge to try to get your pleasure and approval by doing what you ask on the priority things you have selected. High expectations that she can be sensible and cooperative will show that you trust her and are more likely to produce the results that you want.

Step Six

Develop her self-esteem and confidence. Help her to feel better about herself and give her a positive self-image. Put into practice 'The Expertise' (see Chapter Five).

Some further suggestions once you are under way

A human relationship is a very special, complex and finely balanced thing. When it is badly fractured, like a shattered antique vase, repairing it can require skill and patience.

Repairing a relationship involves:
- touching the child
- spending time with and enjoying her
- being firm and clear, but friendly and loving
- praising and approving her and what she does and cutting down on criticism
- avoiding the use of questions
- offering a few limited and managed choices

Using touch

Touch is a very powerful tool, with the potential to either heal or hurt. Although touching is usually done silently, it is also a very powerful way to communicate. There is a whole language associated with touch. Provided the contact is not designed to hurt, children love – indeed yearn – to be touched. However, a child who feels hurt, rejected and resentful is very likely to reject the first overtures of touch. He might push you away, or get up and walk away. If he does, do not give up. Remember – do not make conciliation dependent on reciprocation. It takes time to rebuild trust, so the trick is to be subtle and even devious about it; to find ways to get physically close which do not involve a big statement and which do not require him to return the gesture. In other words, it is best to start with 'giving' touches and not with 'giving and taking' or reciprocated touches.

Examples of two-way, 'giving and taking' touches are body embraces, holding hands, walking arm in arm, even shaking hands.

Examples of one-way, 'giving' touches include:
- sitting beside them while they watch television

- casual body touches as a welcome when you see them after an absence, e.g., after school
- sitting next to them in the car, if changing the regular pattern does not seem too strange
- sharing a bath if they are of an appropriate age
- sitting or lying on their bed next to them at bedtime

Never reject their touch or physical demonstrations of affection – even if they have just been diabolical. If they have made you angry, tell them in words what it is they have done which you did not like. Rejecting their physical advances will convey that it is them, and not their behaviour, that you dislike. Rejecting their physical gestures of need and apology – a complex mix of emotions which it will be impossible for them to express in words – will erect yet another protective barrier and make the reconciliation harder to achieve and even further away.

If they give you a 'giving' touch, make sure you reciprocate. Accept their olive branch, if that is what it is, and acknowledge and meet their need for you and your approval.

Time with them and for them

When the relationship is fractured, at the beginning the time you spend with and for the child must be on his terms. This won't always be easy. Young children need to play. It has been said that children use play much as adults use clothes – as the outward expression of their inner selves. Playing what they want to play means that you accept them as they are. But parents do not always find it easy to play. Although most of us played in our own childhood, we often forget how to do it, or feel uncomfortable doing it. Take the lead from your child. Talk to him about what he is doing. Do not take it over.

Older children 'play' in different ways. They do not play with dolls or cars or building bricks any more. Perhaps the best way to re-establish communication with an older child is to sit with him while he watches his favourite television programme, watch him play football in the park, or ask him to show you how he does whatever it is he takes pride in. Again, it must start by being on his terms, doing things which he likes to do. If you have already listed the likes and dislikes of your child as was suggested earlier, you should be able to identify the point from which, gently, to build bridges.

Beware sabotage!

Like touch, giving your time must be done sensitively. We can apply the same idea of one-way and two-way touching to time. Giving time on your child's terms and asking for nothing in return is a one-way time gift. Reciprocal, or two-way giving of time is inviting him to do something with you which you like to do, in which he has to actively participate with you.

Where there have been many arguments and many disappointments, there will inevitably be mistrust. If you create expectations for your time together which are too high, and if you make your child take equal or more responsibility for making a success of the time, there is a chance that he will sabotage it, refuse to cooperate and make it fail, to protect himself against the disappointment of it possibly ending in breakdown as on previous occasions. Saying something like: *'I think we need to spend some happy time together. I have arranged for your sister to visit a friend so that we can be alone. What would you like to do?'* puts enormous pressure on the child to keep things calm. He may respond by saying he wants to do something which does not involve you – thus defeating the objective – or he may quickly engineer a row to end the uncertainty – thus avoiding the responsibility. If you recognise the pattern, be patient. It is common and understandable. You have to begin again by offering one-way time and attention to demonstrate your commitment, because his trust in you being there for him has been undermined.

Examples of one-way time for your child, time which does not require him to do anything in return, are:

- read to him
- watch him as he is doing what he enjoys or is good at, e.g., sports, tree-climbing
- do things in parallel, so talking is not necessary and nothing is at stake. Do your chores in the same room where he is doing something else, provided it is not his bedroom. Conversely, you could invite him to join you and keep you company

Be firm and clear, but friendly and loving

Make statements. Keep them short. If you use explanations, use as few as possible – if one will do, just use that and say nothing more. Don't use 'floppy' phrases such as 'I think', 'perhaps', 'maybe'. 'Please' is friendly, but sometimes gets the answer 'no'. Use it carefully.

State clearly what it is that you want to happen: *'I am letting you know now that when we go to the shops today, I shall not be buying you any sweets or toys. This is a shopping expedition for our food, not for anything else.'* And stick to it. It means that you have to think ahead about the problems which may arise, and build a plan. But it will be time well invested.

Continue to give plenty of praise and approval
Say you like what he does, you like who he is and you like being with him.

Avoid unnecessary questions
Questions need answers. They are best avoided, because both questions and the answers to them can be used inappropriately as tools of power.

Using questions as power
Questions need answers and demand attention. They can therefore be intrusive and put people on the defensive. Adults frequently use questions to control children, to seek information children might not want to give, and to get information on their terms. Too many questions can cause resentment. Always use the 'Need to Know Test'. Ask yourself before you speak: do I really need to know that?

Snooping questions. Children should be allowed autonomy: some space in their lives in which they are accountable only to themselves. This is particularly true of their thoughts. Although it is sometimes fascinating to know what is going on in their heads, much of the time that is nobody's business but theirs. They have to be allowed to grow in their own way. Asking too many snooping questions will serve only to inhibit growth by making them feel untrustworthy.

Trip-wire questions. Asking a question to which you already know the answer is a power tactic which can cause enormous resentment, especially if your prior knowledge is discovered. If you know the answer, do not ask the question.

Instead of *'What have you been doing here?'* you can say *'I can see that you have been drawing on your brother's book!'* Using questions to catch them out is also unhelpful because they will feel manipulated.

Put-down questions. Parents often use questions to which they do not really expect an answer, to 'rub their child's nose' in a failure. For example, *'Why are you so stupid?'* or *'Why are you so clumsy?'* are both much more demeaning than *'That was a clumsy/stupid thing to do.'*

Using answers as power

Asking a question immediately hands the initiative to the person who is going to answer. It puts them centre-stage and potentially gives them enormous scope to choose between compliance and disruption, to set or change the agenda.

- Asking a question gives the idea that there is a choice of action when there is none. *'Shall we go up to bed now?'* is probably not what you really mean!
- Out of the choices which are available, you might get the answer you realise only then that you *really* did not want.
- Asking questions and giving choices sometimes gives the impression that you are unclear about what should be happening. That is why you are asking. Remember, don't be floppy.
- Being given the chance to answer is an invitation to the child to offer a challenge and say he wants the opposite. It allows him to retake control.
- A child who is feeling insecure will want the parent to be decisive, to take the responsibility and not to pass it over. Answers require the respondent to make a statement, to

make a stand and be clear about things. The child is not always ready for that. Questions such as '*Are you feeling fed up today?*' are discomforting. He will not know which is the best answer to give, tactically or otherwise. It might lead to another question, '*Why?*', which he almost certainly will wish to avoid. If, instead, you use a statement such as '*I can see that today you are feeling fed up about something*', it allows him to continue feeling fed up, and be relieved that you have understood.

Choices

Limited and managed choices give the opportunity for autonomy. If your child has been trying to take control, then he may feel resentful and fearful about all his control being taken away at once. Giving him limited opportunities to decide things for himself will help not only to offset any feelings of fear or even panic that he has lost control, but also to take some responsibility for himself and to establish a picture of who he is. Choices about things which are particularly personal, for example what clothes to wear or how to spend his time, are therefore most appropriate at the beginning. As he becomes more accommodating and trust-worthy, the scope for choice can be extended.

Giving choices involves asking questions and seems, therefore, to go against the advice offered in the previous section. The emphasis must be on both *limited* and *managed* choices.

Managed choice means that you decide what options your child is given to choose between, making sure that you will be happy with whichever choice he makes. For example, on a cold day you may ask, '*Would you like to wear your tracksuit or jeans and a jumper?*' instead of the open question '*What*

would you like to wear today?' which might produce an unsuitable answer. If that degree of choice leads to confrontation, it may be appropriate to offer only a choice of socks: *'Would you like the blue or the red socks today?'*

Limited choice means you keep the opportunities for even managed choice to a few times a day. As his behaviour stabilises and his sense of security increases, the number of choices can be increased. It will be important gradually to extend the choices, for children as well as adults need to develop a sense of autonomy and have some scope for self-determination.

Managing deadlock and defiance: achieving agreement and compliance without playing power

Management training for people in senior positions as leaders or negotiators contains a great deal of advice on how to reach agreement in ways which keep all the people involved happy. Much of this advice can be applied to the relationship between parent and child. There is, however, an important difference between the two situations. In many areas of management, the other party has a right to reject the solution or walk away from it if it does not suit them. Solutions cannot be imposed. The aim, therefore, is to reach agreement. For parents, the objective is to achieve compliance. Agreement is desirable but not necessary. Ultimately, we can and often do require that children meet our demands whether they like them or not. We are in a position of power, and we have the ultimate deterrent of positive sanctions (e.g., bribes or other rewards) and negative sanctions (e.g., punishments) available to get our way. However, the aim must always be to get compliance using our authority and other methods before we have to resort to sanctions, which are the tools of power.

Despite this difference, there is a lot to learn from the techniques and analyses offered to managers. After all, we are looking at the same kind of skills – people skills. As has been discussed earlier in this chapter, power solutions should be used as little as possible because they establish unhelpful, tit-for-tat-style practices and patterns; they pass on bad habits and unhelpful social skills to children; and they generally end up damaging the parent–child relationship. So what are the key ways of achieving compliance? How can we best manage our children to minimise the amount of conflict and negative power play and maximise the positive experiences of parenting?

There are four basic ways to get compliance. These are through:
- trust
- reason
- creativity
- power and sanctions

Trust
A child who feels trusted by an adult tends to feel proud of that trust so she likes to live up to the expectations that adult has of her to strengthen it. All the research on human behaviour shows that high expectations of performance produce good results, and low expectations produce poor results, hence the common phrase, 'What you see is what you get'. What you see is, in this case, your perception of your child's personality and behaviour. What you get is the behaviour you expect. It is another way to describe the self-

fulfilling prophecy. So, if you ask a child to do things in a way that assumes and expects that she will, you are more likely to have her comply. The same is true with the reverse – when you let slip that you think she will not do as you want.

For example, *'Time for school in ten minutes. Remember what you need and I'll see you at the front door at quarter to'* is better than *'You've only got ten minutes. Have you got your homework, have you done your teeth, don't forget your games kit, and don't be late like yesterday!'*

Without realising it, we often use forms of words that undermine the trust, which show that we are actually not sure that a child will be able to carry out what we ask. Above is an elaborate example. More often, we just slip in the one-word question, 'Promise?' and pop goes the trust.

Seeking a promise to back up the commitment to deliver undermines your child's belief in your trust, it destroys the expectation that, naturally, she will be able to achieve what you have asked and, of itself, plants the idea of non-compliance. It may even be seen as a challenge and could spur defiance. This is the most common way the 'trust' strategy can backfire. Another is that the expectations you have may be too ambitious. A promise or expectation that is hard to deliver sets the child up to fail. Make sure, then, that the expectation is realistic and age-appropriate.

What happens if you show trust, keep your expectations sensible, but your child still fails to deliver? For example, she is still not getting up early enough to avoid last-minute panic before school, continues to forget her homework or swimming kit, her clothes still lie in piles over the bedroom floor? What can you do then? Should you start nagging and reminding again? *No.*

Before you return to that you could:

- put her further in charge and give her *more* responsibility. For example, give her an alarm clock so you do not have to wake her up; give her peel-off notepads which she can use to remind herself
- let her 'face the music', be late, leave things behind, go to school in her pyjamas (yes, this is what one mother did at the teacher's suggestion and the child never refused to get dressed again!), leave homework undone – learning the hard way is often foolish, but sometimes it is the most effective way
- work out a system or routine together which will help her to remember tasks and responsibilities

Note: If you trust, and expect compliance, and your child in turn trusts you to behave fairly and broadly in her interests, this amounts to you exercising your authority and her accepting it.

Reason

Getting agreement or compliance using reason is highly desirable. Rather than merely issuing decrees and demanding that your will be done, like a dictator, this strategy involves giving reasons for asking the child to do particular things. The request is therefore seen as reasonable and sensible, and its and your purpose is understood. Giving reasons not only teaches children to be rational – that it is appropriate to be able and willing to account for behaviour, and to recognise what constitute strong and weak reasons – but it also shows that you respect their right to know.

The tendency to treat children as people with rights, interests and feelings is the great advance in child-rearing in recent times. This lies at the heart of the child-centred approach championed by the famous child psychologists of the 1960s and 70s and which is now being called into question by people who wish to turn the clock back and 'bring back discipline'. It may seem difficult to understand how this eminently civilised approach to the parent–child relationship can go wrong. But it can. And it largely has. It is important to understand why it does not always work, so that its misapplication can be corrected and the vital elements of it can be retained and not thrown out in any return to the idea of children being seen but not heard.

What can go wrong?

The problem is that too much emphasis on reason can lead to too much talk, which can obscure, manipulate and confuse rather than clarify. Young children, especially, cannot cope with complex argument and logic. Words can be used to entangle and manipulate and can very easily become tools of power. Every child under the age of, say, ten will be at a disadvantage with just about every adult when it comes to a verbal competition. Once power is seen as the name of the game, children will dig in their heels, using their own power tactics, and clashes will inevitably follow.

Explanation or persuasion?

Even with older children, the 'rational' approach can misfire. If more than one or two reasons are given to explain a request, they not only open the door to counterarguments, but also can appear as attempts to persuade the child – which automatically gives him the opportunity to remain unpersuaded. Persuasion implies a right of veto. And what if he says no?

Keep the boundaries clear

First and foremost, it is important to keep the boundaries – the rules and requirements – clear. If reason gets the upper hand, and you listen and accommodate too much to counter-reasons, the boundaries are likely to be adjusted and qualified so much that children never really know where they stand or what is expected of them.

How to cut down on the 'verbals'

- State your reasons briefly and firmly. Use only one or two strong arguments, even if there are more. Then stay quiet and wait, expectantly.
- Give reasons the child will understand.
- Beware justifying the reasons further. Think (but don't say!): do I *really* need to justify myself to a . . .-year-old?
- Use silence, facial expression and gentle and directive touch more. A gentle ushering, hands on shoulders, in the direction of the bedroom can say a final 'Upstairs now' more convincingly than the words repeated yet again.

Note: If you give one or two reasons only as explanation, rather than persuasion or justification, you are in effect exercising your authority – rationally and not dictatorially. You are saying, gently: this is what I expect, this is why, now go and do it.

Creativity

Creative solutions to deadlock and defiance defuse or divert attention from the (usually quite petty) issue at hand, allowing parent, child or both to get things back in proportion and climb down without loss of face. Both sides can get caught in a battle of wills in which the potential damage to the relationship far outweighs the importance of the matter in dispute. Try to remember that you are the adult – which should not be interpreted as giving you the right to win – which means that you have both the ability to keep the issue in perspective, to look beyond the moment, and the responsibility and maturity to know when enough is enough and to bring it to an end.

Tactics for defusing deadlock include:
- changing the subject
- making things fun
- compromise
- humour

Changing the subject

We are all capable of getting wound up about things: when we force an issue, find arguments to use for argument's sake, and take the issue much further than we ever intended. Children do the same. When your child is winding you up, perhaps just to get your attention, it is far better to ignore it and talk about something completely different, or suggest doing something together to get the issue dropped. Trying to 'win' the argument, or rising to the challenge of a minor insult, will only stir up trouble. Showing that you are unmoved by his challenges may even mean that he eventually gives them up.

Making things fun

Car journeys, shopping trips and collecting brothers and sisters from school can be made fun. For example, on any walk you can count how many front doors of different colours or cats and dogs that you pass. You can count how many manhole covers you see. Car journeys can be made livelier by collecting pub names or makes of car.

Compromise

Compromise is a situation in which both parties get something (the important bits) of what they want but not all of it. It is therefore a 'win–win' outcome. Compromise is a gesture of strength, not of weakness. Provided it creates an alternative which genuinely meets everyone's interests, and is not a disguise for a climbdown by the parent, it is a creative way out of, or to avoid, deadlock. It shows respect for the interests of the child, will enhance his self-esteem, and will give him problem-solving skills which he can use immediately to his advantage when playing with brothers and sisters or with friends at home and at school. (See Chapter Five, 'The Expertise'.)

Humour

See the funny side of the often ridiculous situation you are both caught up in. Laugh at yourself, or gently at both of you – but never at the child alone! Laughter and humour are great natural remedies; great tools for releasing tension.

How can this strategy go wrong?

Creative solutions can also backfire unless carefully deployed. Children sometimes need to do what they are told, and quickly, especially if their safety is threatened. If they are frequently allowed to wriggle their way out of a straight demand, one day they might find themselves facing danger. Another problem is that they can learn and adopt the same techniques and not always use them at the right times. They can certainly exhaust you with their ingenuity when the last thing you feel like is a long-winded discussion of all the alternatives.

Children can, therefore, get wise to your game because, like reasons, compromises can be manipulative. For a while, you will always have better ideas than they will. Make sure that *their* creativity is not manipulation, a version of power play, expressing a need always to retain some control of events.

While compromise (win–win) is desirable, climbdown (win–lose) is not. Beware of dressing up your capitulation as compromise to make it seem acceptable. A rough guide to tell which you are doing might be how soon the 'compromise' option develops. The sooner you hit upon it, the more genuine it will be. The later it appears, the more potential there is for manipulation and giving in.

What can you do if your child finds straight demands difficult? To be able to argue, to make critical judgements and to identify concessions are very valuable skills for children to develop. Just as important, though, is the sense to recognise when these responses are not appropriate – when it is simplest and best to accept the boundary where it is and not to start the negotiation process. Parents can help their children to develop this by:

- Compromising less. It is sensible to be flexible on the issues about which a child feels strongly, such as being able to do her favourite activity. However, on lesser or unimportant issues it will be wise to stick to what was previously agreed or to insist that what you want to happen takes place.
- Acknowledging the child's interests and feelings even if you are not taking them into account this time. His

resentment at being overridden will be lessened if he feels that you know and understand how he is feeling and why he is reacting that way to your demand.

Power and the use of sanctions (punishments and rewards)

Ultimately, parents can always resort to the use of power tactics to impose their will. Sometimes this is appropriate, but sometimes it is not. We have to find the right balance between staying 'in charge', but not getting caught up in power battles to prove it.

The key thing is to use our authority sparingly, concentrating on the important issues such as children's safety and behaving decently to others – us included. If we get into the habit of controlling many areas of their lives, using either punishments, shouting or threats and bribes, the strategy is very likely to backfire. We may end up losing our power, our authority and our self-respect as well.

How can this strategy go wrong?

- We may not realise that things like threats and bribes, or shouting and shaming, are forms of power which children grow to resent deeply.
- We may not appreciate that power tactics are often a challenge to misbehaviour because it allows the child to stay in control.
- If power tactics are used too often they become easier to ignore and invite power responses.

Relying on power, either physical or emotional, is counterproductive. It is temporary because there comes a time when power runs out; and it is, usually, emotionally damaging to the child.

How can you unravel the tangle if it does go wrong?
When you find yourself in constant power battles, you must change the ground rules for the relationship. Stop using the tools of power and instead rely on your parental authority.

- Try getting compliance through using trust, reason, creativity and understanding.
- It will be important to reduce the number of fights. Choose only one or two negative behaviours to work on at a time.
- Try to stop shouting and issuing threats and conditions. Try what some people call the 'soft no'. Instead of getting louder and louder, the demand should be said quieter and quieter, looking the child in the eye as you say it.
- If you mean business, you must use the right body language. This means standing face to face with the child; stopping what else you are doing while you say no; and staying still while you wait for him to carry out the demand.
- Sometimes, you need to gently direct him – lift him out of the bath, usher him to his bedroom, or in through the front door.
- Give him choices to help him feel back in control of his own life.
- Spend time with your child to help him realise that you care.

(See also 'Getting started', page 66.)

4

Where Do You Fit In?

At the same time as looking after our children, we have to look after ourselves. If we don't, the job of bringing up children will be much less enjoyable and therefore harder than it need be. We have to start with learning to be comfortable and happy with ourselves. We have to understand our own need for play, praise, love and growth, go at least some way to meeting those needs and learn to accept ourselves as we are. Only then can we freely and unthreateningly love our children, and accept them as they are. Children, and even small babies, must always be seen as whole people. If we can learn to be more aware of ourselves and what makes us feel good or perform at our best, that is the most important route to understanding our children and getting the best out of them.

No human being is sufficiently saintly to be able to think about someone else's interests all the time to the exclusion of their own. Nor should this even be thought of as a desirable state of affairs. Children demand and need a great deal of time and attention. Giving as much as they sometimes want takes a lot out of you. Indeed, they can take so much out that you often wonder whether there is anything left of you. If you do not consciously take the time regularly to replenish yourself, to recharge your batteries, in other words to take time out for you and to develop your own self-esteem, you can find yourself putting up protective barriers around yourself in a desperate and arbitrary way. You may be holding on to yourself, but you might also be cutting yourself off from your child when, or especially when, your child needs you most and you feel most drained.

The best way to help your children grow up happy and healthy is to make sure that you continue to develop throughout this time and that there is something in it for you. That doesn't always happen smoothly or quite to plan, because what you are able to do with or for one child, you won't be able to do for the next. All of this is inevitable.

The most sensible thing to do about this is to accept from the beginning that you must make space in your life for you. 'Pie in the sky!' many may say, but it needn't be. The important thing is not to try to achieve too much at the wrong time. Of course, we all know that the most trying times for anyone with small children is when it is hardest to get away – when your baby is small and if you are breast-feeding; when your children are so young they spend most of the day at home; and in the late afternoon, between tea and bedtime. But at those times, even a very short break doing something that you like doing, that corresponds with your image of yourself or makes you feel good and indulged can make the world of difference. What all mums need is a bit of 'respite' care!

You need to work on your own self-esteem at the same

time as nurturing your child's; to attend to your own personal growth while you help your child to grow. You can't put yourself into cold storage or on to the back burner for the duration. Why? Very simply, because:

- when you are feeling good, you are nicer to everyone around you
- when you become aware of what makes you feel good, and how good you can feel when things are going right for you, it gives you a much better insight into how to help your child to feel the same way
- the more there is in your life, the more you can demonstrate to your child by example how much there is 'out there' to enjoy – they may even take an interest in, and so share, what so obviously interests you
- the more there is in your life, the less you are there as a door mat for everyone else's convenience and the more you are able to teach them to respect other people's needs, space and general personal boundaries.

WHAT IS YOUR LITTLE LUXURY? WHAT MAKES YOU FEEL GOOD?

- When others tell you that you look nice?
- Reading a good trashy book?
- Going to the pictures?
- Reading a newspaper or magazine?
- Going to the shops and buying something, small (tights or magazine) or large (beware!)?
- Having a long, scented or foamy bath, uninterrupted?
- Going for a walk in the park at *your* pace, and not having to talk to a single child?

- When your partner comes and gives you a large and spontaneous hug?
- Sitting and having a cup of tea and a gossip with your best friend?
- Going out on your own to town, just to walk around and see other 'grown-up' people leading 'normal' lives?
- Going to a bar with your partner or friend?

For each person, the chosen thing will be different, precisely because you are unique. What you choose defines who you are. It's entirely up to you to decide. No one else can, or should, do it for you. And the fact that you make a choice also gives you a sense of being in control of *your* life. It would be hard to underestimate the beneficial effect of feeling that you are, once again, in control of yourself.

What's the pattern?

Instead of seeing your choices about how you would like to spend a free afternoon as a series of one-off, unconnected episodes, you may find it useful to see if they conform to a pattern. If they do, then you can begin to think of other things to do which, for example, may take less time or money and be easier to set up.

- Do you like to end up with something to talk about, a topic of conversation other than babies, to help you appear more interesting to your partner or socially confident with others?
- Is it praise from a special, or any, source which gives you the lift?

- Is it doing something on your own, making you realise you can still survive in the big wide world out there?
- Is it other adult company, uninterrupted by a little person's toilet needs and pestering, which you crave?
- Is it doing something energetic or physical which revitalises you – doing keep fit, playing tennis, going for a swim or a run?
- Do you only feel really good when others say nice things about you? (A reality, but it can be dangerous!) Try to be more in control of when it happens!

Seeing a pattern also helps you to be aware of the kind of person you are, making it easier to reassert your identity.

Beware!
- Choose something achievable. Grandiose schemes, unless very well organised, are often doomed to fail and this will have the opposite of the desired effect.
- Don't put it off because there is not enough time. Write down, say, four or six different time periods – five minutes, fifteen minutes, one hour, two hours, half a day, a whole day, covering what realistically may be available to you – and fill in what you could or would like to do in each of them. When one of the time holes opens up, fill it with the task or activity appropriate to it, e.g., *'I've got ten minutes spare. That's my time slot for putting some make-up on/reading the front page of the newspaper . . .'*
- If possible, set it up to happen on a regular basis. This might mean organising a childminding swap with a friend, asking your mother to come over and babysit, or

getting the children in the bath five minutes early. While some things which make you feel good can be slotted into small time slots which just appear, others need more time and therefore need to be planned for.

- Don't choose something which acts counter to any other goal or requirement in your life because it will then have little long-term benefit and will only make you feel guilty or a failure later. For example, don't choose going out to have a coffee and cake with a friend if you are always trying to lose weight. Don't choose going out and spending money on yourself if you usually have to live within a tight budget.

- You may feel that you would want to choose to do something with your partner. However, if the exercise is designed to help you get a clear picture of who you are and what makes you feel good, it is probably advisable to pick on at least one thing to do which has nothing to do with a regular partner.

'I've always wanted to . . .'
So do it! Go for it!

But who am I?
If you can't think of anything to do which says something significant about you and which you are happy to identify with, think back to the things you used to enjoy doing in 'life before children'. Although as time goes by the new experiences we have mean that we change and develop, those same experiences can cause us, sometimes, to leave a part of ourselves behind. See if it is possible to resurrect old interests and rediscover that buried, but not lost, identity.

How can I help my child to be strong and confident if I'm so unsure about myself?

It is sometimes said that if a parent does not have self-esteem, it cannot be transmitted to a child. This defeatist or negative statement makes one important mistake. It assumes that self-esteem exists as a constant quantity throughout the whole of one's life, instead of seeing it as something which fluctuates and changes, something which can be topped up or drawn down. It rather assumes that either you have it or you don't; and that if you have it, you have it in a fixed amount.

Neither life nor human beings are like that. We all have times when we feel stronger and more confident, and times when we feel less able to cope or feel we have nothing to offer. When we feel good about ourselves, we are less vulnerable to other people's criticism, but we are not immune to being undermined if the criticism is continuous, is from a particularly valued person or is particularly cruel. Self-esteem can, therefore, be undermined or boosted. There is little point in trying to work out, if indeed that is possible, how much self-esteem you or your child has. There are, of course, no appropriate units of measurement. The key point is that, in virtually every situation we experience, someone else can make quite a difference to how good or bad we feel about ourselves. And how we feel about ourselves, to repeat the key message of this book, influences significantly how we behave towards and interact with other people. As adults, we also have the ability, to an extent, to control it ourselves. Not only should we have a better idea of what does give us a boost, we also are in a much better position to make it happen. We are much more in charge of our own time. The responsibility for breaking out of any downward spiral lies with us. It is up to us, the adult, to lift both ourselves and our children to a point where we no longer need to taunt or deflate them, or 'put them down', in order to protect ourselves.

5

A Way to Remember the Key Points:

'THE EXPERTISE'

WHAT IS 'THE EXPERTISE'?

'The Expertise' is not something that only the 'experts' or 'professionals' have. It is, instead, something that you have within you, within your grasp. From the beginning, this book has tried to persuade parents to trust themselves, to pay attention to who they are and to do it their way. You are the expert on you and your child. 'The Expertise' is, instead, really a collection of tools for the job – a technique both for remembering the key points to help you decide what to do in any particular situation and a guide to what you need to do for yourself to keep you sane and help you to develop yourself.

Each tool relates to a syllable, individual letter or pair of letters in the word 'Expertise', as follows:

EXPERTISE *Ex*plain, *Ex*ample
EX*P*ERTISE *P*raise, *P*eace, *P*lay
EXPER*T*ISE *T*rust, *T*ouch, *T*ime, *T*alk
EXPERT*ISE* Empath*ise*, Sympath*ise*, Apolog*ise*, Comprom*ise*

Each of these 'tools' will be discussed in turn; and each discussion covers both how to use this tool to help your child, and how to apply it to yourself, to boost your own self-esteem. Looking after yourself, as we have already seen, will not only make you feel better. It will also help you to appreciate how effective these key concepts are for improving self-image, and make you more committed to applying them to your child.

*EX*PLAIN; *EX*AMPLE

*Ex*plain

If you explain things to your child you show that you:
- respect her right to know
- empathise with her need to make sense of her immediate world
- respect her ability to comprehend and understand
- trust her

One of the most important needs we all have is to be kept informed about things that affect us. We get extremely annoyed if employers, partners, schools or neighbours do things which affect our lives without consulting us or, at the very least, warning us. Children, of course, have less experience of life and people to help them to anticipate what might happen or what might be the consequences of certain events. They will therefore feel *more* confused, uncertain and insecure than adults would if they are not told when, why or for how long things will be different. If you do not give your children explanations, they will suffer.

They will live in an environment which seems arbitrary. They will be unable, therefore, to predict anything about their life and cannot possibly develop any sense of security in their relations with the outside world. They will feel vulnerable and will work out ways to protect themselves from the discomfort of uncertainty. They may withdraw, learn to control others, which is the closest they can get to controlling their circumstances, or control themselves by developing rigid, inflexible patterns for their own behaviour.

They will find it difficult to get a sense of their own worth. It will be difficult for them to believe themselves to be important if no one else bothers to keep them informed of changes, events or decisions affecting themselves or key people around them, or if no one seems interested in offering an opportunity for them to state their reactions to the changes, events or decisions.

What sort of things should be explained to children?
Children should know about:
- events
- feelings
- changes
- decisions
- facts

Events
- Before: what is going to happen (i.e., preparation for an event). Even babies can be told that they are about to be

taken out shopping, to go up to the bath, to go to collect their brothers and sisters from school. Even if they do not understand, your voice will be reassuring. You can even sing a little tune for each separate event so they can know what is about to happen without needing to understand language.

- During: why something is happening.
- After: why something happened (i.e., after the event, if it was unexpected).

Feelings
- how you are feeling
- how you imagine they are feeling

Changes
- absences
- routines
- partners/friends

Decisions
- Explain the reason for your decision. Do not give too many reasons because they may then appear as persuasion.

Facts
- If children ask for information about something, you should answer, or try to find out the answer if you do not already know it. *'Stop asking all those questions!'* is not the right reaction.
- Less comfortable facts of life such as death or divorce should be dealt with honestly in terms which the particular child can most comfortably comprehend.

Should we explain everything?

Age-appropriateness

If a child asks for an explanation about something, however difficult it might be, he should be told something which at least approximates to the truth. You do not have to give long or full explanations. But distorting the truth should be avoided. There are some very good children's books telling stories that involve some sensitive issues such as going to hospital, dying, divorce or moving. Anyone who feels uncomfortable talking directly to their child about these things can always go to a local library and ask to borrow the relevant books. The issue can be raised through reading the story. It may take time and effort to make the journey, but it will be time well invested because children, like adults, hate to be kept in the dark.

Explanation and you

If it is not obvious why something happened – why you had a row with someone, for example, or why you did not feel like doing something when someone asked you to – try asking yourself why. Looking at various explanations will help you to get closer to your own feelings and moods. Doing this will, in turn, help you to get closer to the feelings of others around you, including your child.

Ask another person involved why something happened. If you are genuinely puzzled by another person's behaviour or reaction, get used to asking them why. There might be a simple explanation. Once you realise the good feeling you get when you know and understand things that are happening to you, you will be in a better position to see how much better your child will feel when he is forewarned or is able to understand.

Be cautious about asking a child why he did something. (See 'Using questions as power', page 73.)

Example

From the moment of birth children learn from us. From our responses to them they learn what it is that they do which pleases us – their smiles, for example. They also copy our behaviour directly, both because they want to be like those whom they love and because they cannot help it. It happens without us being aware of it. They copy gestures and opinions, and absorb values and attitudes. Children learn, good or bad, more from us than from anywhere else, even school or television. As they get older and they are able to judge and evaluate for themselves, the influence of the parents diminishes. There are many different reasons for this. But the influence will remain potent, none the less.

Parents set an example in many aspects of life and living, some more important than others. For example, children will watch parents and any other carers and observe:

- how they treat people
- how they spend their time
- their attitudes to a whole range of things
- their view of what is right and wrong
- how they handle frustration
- how they solve problems

'Do as I say, not as I do!'

It is an unpleasant truth that children pay little attention when we ask them to do something that we are not willing to do ourselves. And why should they?

- Why should they stop hitting their siblings if you hit them as a punishment for doing it?
- Why should they not be allowed to shout at you if you do it to them?
- Why should they not watch television as their main leisure activity if that is how you spend much of your free time?
- If you snack throughout the day, how can you expect them to stick to eating only at meal times?
- If you are bad-tempered much of the time, how can you ask for or expect others around you to be controlled and respectful?
- If you do not put yourself out to help them or others, why should they feel like helping you?

Whatever it is that we want them to do or to achieve, we have to make sure we apply the same standards to ourselves. This is very difficult. We may try to excuse ourselves and admit that we made a mistake in doing something, and that we do not want them to make the same mistake, or go through the same learning curve. But it will not sound very convincing. They might reply, with some justification, that they wish to be left to make their own mistakes.

If we want our children to do certain things, most of us go about achieving this through nagging and criticism. But nagging and criticism sow doubt and resentment. It is far more effective to live by our words and behave as we want them to. We need to be the model instead of the critic.

Example and you

If we want children to do things which we find difficult, how can we begin to set a better example? We can try the 'contract approach'. This involves accepting and defining where both parties' performance falls short and setting targets for both sides to improve. The honesty and the shared effort will bring parties closer together, often with laughs in the process. The alternative, nagging option, by contrast, opens up chasms.

PRAISE; PEACE; PLAY

Praise

It is good practice to:
- find one thing to praise every day
- praise the deed rather than the person
- praise the process rather than the product

Most people respond better to praise than to criticism. Yet despite knowing this, far too many of us find it easier to find fault and to judge than to give support and approval. Part of the problem is that we are out of the habit of giving praise. There is also a tendency to think that praise and approval will make our children big-headed. But the reality would seem to go deeper than either of these partial explanations. Criticism is a negative judgement. It puts the person doing the judging in a superior and slightly distant position, which gives the impression of authority. Praising someone, on the other hand, implies a sense of equality and involves giving, and therefore getting close. It is a far more uncomfortable thing to do.

What do we mean by 'praise'?

Praise can take different forms, and mean slightly different things. The dictionary defines praise as: 'express warm approbation of; commend the merits of'. 'Praise' therefore, can mean both 'approval' and 'appreciation'.

What is the difference between the two words, and is it important?

Approve is defined as: 'confirm, accept, commend'.

Appreciate is defined as: 'estimate worth, quality, amount of; be sensitive to; esteem highly'.

In other words, 'approval' implies the whole-hearted acceptance – of the person, or of something which that person has done – without considering or evaluating in any detail why we accept that person or their product. 'Appreciation' is about worth, and valuing different qualities, especially effort. The difference between 'approval' and 'appreciation' is important. Children need to feel approved of for who they are, and appreciated for their efforts and skills.

What can we praise?

We can praise:

- helpfulness
- thoughtfulness
- effort
- ideas
- skills
- choices
- independence

The language of praise: descriptive praise

Praise the deed rather than the person.

It is very easy, and very common, to use the word 'good', in relation to children. It is short, convenient, but what does it mean?

Instead of 'good', you can say 'clever', 'thoughtful', 'thanks for doing that', 'sensible', 'helpful when I needed help'.

Approval words

- That's lovely!
- That's great!
- Well done!
- Brilliant!
- You're a star!
- I'm so impressed!

Appreciation words

- Thank you for doing that.
- That was a great help to me.
- You took a lot of time and care over that.

For example, you could say:

CLOTHES

'*That was a good choice of clothes to put on today, given the weather*', '*Those things go nicely together*' (instead of '*What a good boy to get yourself dressed!*')

IDEAS

'*It was clever to think of doing it that way*', '*What a great idea for a game*' (instead of '*You are good to have gone off and played*')

 104 A WAY TO REMEMBER THE KEY POINTS

EFFORT

'You really tried hard', 'You did well to get so far/to do so much', 'That model must have taken you a long time' (instead of 'That's a good model')

HELPFULNESS

'Thanks for tidying away your toys', 'It was great that you got yourself ready for bed tonight as I am very tired', 'Getting tea ready with me was a great help. Thanks' (instead of 'You are so good')

INDEPENDENCE

'You can do things very well on your own now', 'I knew that you'd be able to do that', 'You tried so hard to do up those buttons. You must feel really proud you cracked it' (instead of 'Good boy to do up your buttons')

THOUGHTFULNESS

'I saw you help that little boy with his shoes in the park. That was kind' (instead of 'I saw your good deed')

SKILLS

'That was brilliant how you did that! You're so clever at that sort of thing', 'You can kick a ball a long way now', 'You played well with Gemma given you'd never met her before. You're good at making friends' (instead of 'You're a good footballer')

Children's art and crafts

If your child goes to a playgroup or nursery, the chances are that she will come home every week with armfuls of paintings, drawings and, most beloved by the collecting adults, still sticky and decidedly fragile junk models. These creations are very important (see 'Play', page 114). How should you respond to these labours of love? What should you actually say? Do you lie through your teeth and declare them all to be worthy of hanging in a gallery? Should you be honest and say what you really feel about them? Should you try and identify what they are? Should you keep *all* of them, or 'bin' them as soon as her back is turned? And should you offer any advice on how to make a tree look more like a tree, or point out that, in fact, there is a neck between people's heads and bodies? If your child is the only one not coming home with dripping paintings or sticky models, does it matter?

'Are you pleased with it?'

Whatever it is she has done, especially if it is something that she is asking you to comment on, one way to respond is to turn it back to her and ask her what she thinks. Ultimately, children have to do things for their own satisfaction or to meet their own objectives, and not because it pleases us. Of course, they will want us to be pleased by their efforts; and it is more important to comment on the effort than on what they have produced. But if you say something is 'good', and your child does not agree, she will see your praise as false. Your approval will not help her. If, on the other hand, she is already pleased with it, you need to let her know that that is enough – that your opinion is not as important as her own. Gradually, and increasingly, she will thus learn to value and trust her own judgements and attitudes.

Is all praise good? No!

When parents do praise children, or declare their love for them, sometimes without realising it they can say things that do not, in fact, make the child feel good about herself or about what she has done. Although it is true that we do not, generally, praise enough, we need to be aware that praise is not always *well meant* or well received and may be ignored or rejected.

Praise which is not always well meant: manipulative praise and emotional blackmail

Saying *'I love you'* can be another way of praising, or showing approval. But it is sometimes said by parents in order to get something in return, to make the child feel guilty if she does not want to do something being asked of her. *'But I love you. Surely you will do this little thing for me?'* It can then be turned round to become *'If you really loved me, you would not think of doing what you are about to do.'*

Praise which is not always well received: unqualified, false and overfrequent praise

The following conversation between a mother and her two-year-old illustrates one of the problems with unqualified praise.

Mother: I adore you!
Child: Don't adore me, Mummy.
Mother: Why not?
Child: Because I cry too much.

This brief exchange shows how difficult it can be for children to receive unqualified and generalised praise. While we all thrive on praise and appreciation, we receive it comfortably, and it really only rewards us, not only if we feel it is justified but also if we can comfortably keep up that standard. What the little girl in this incident is saying is: '*I cannot have the responsibility of always behaving in the way that pleases you and justifies your love. I am not that good. I cry a lot (which you let me know you do not like).*' If you say to a child instead that you appreciate what she has done, and make it specific to an act or event, or that you love her despite or because of her faults, there is no expectation or responsibility for her to carry on pleasing, delivering and being perfect. No one is perfect. And in any case, perfection is a treadmill.

Children feel many mixed and very strong emotions about people in their family. Adults, who limit freedom and sometimes fail to deliver love when it is needed, stir up plenty of angry feelings. Brothers and sisters are also frequently objects of hatred as they are rivals for attention, approval, possessions and space. Children's fantasy is highly volatile and imaginative. There will be many moments of intense hatred, fear, loathing and resentment when they can wish the worst on those around them. To be told, close to one of these moments of private intrigue and wickedness, that they are 'good' can cause not only guilt and confusion, but also a sense of failure at not being able to live up to expectations. They will also feel a need to hide the wicked bits of themselves. It will be far better to say, '*I bet you wished you could kick your brother then. Well done for only thinking it*' than '*Weren't you good not to hurt your brother today.*'

FALSE PRAISE

Children will see through praise that is patently false. They will be as sensitive to insincerity as we are. However, we all like a little flattery. There is a significant difference between unnecessary praise and false praise. The word 'flattery' is used to cover both forms. Unnecessary praise may be used to get on the good side of someone, but at least it is the truth. False praise is offensive.

Too much praise can not only diminish its value but also encourage children either to become praise-dependent – reliant on someone saying something is satisfactory before they can move on to the next task or project – or to be reluctant to judge things for themselves.

Praise and perfectionism

When children sense they are loved and approved of only when they do well at something that a parent seems to value, not loved unconditionally for who they are, there is the possibility that they will apply undue effort to that activity and strive to be perfect to please, while never being quite sure any particular achievement is really deserving of approval. And in the process of doing well according to someone else's criteria, a child can lose touch with who they are. To avoid an unhealthy perfectionism creeping in, praise should be offered for 'good enough success' and not reserved for only 'the best'.

Praise and presents

Praise is showing appreciation in words. Presents are another way of saying thank you and expressing love. It is a joy to see the surprised delight in a child's eyes when they receive something unexpected. Giving gives us pleasure, too. But presents should not become a substitute for words or non-material gestures. Children value both ways of showing love.

Praise and conceit

Some people feel uncomfortable with the idea of praising their children. For them, it smacks of flattery. We grow up believing that it is better to slap children down, to put them in their place, than to encourage them to have pride in their achievements – in case this encourages conceit.

When a child believes that his particular abilities makes him *better as a person* than others without those talents, and when that belief causes him to *look down on others* and consider them inferior, the child does, indeed, come across as an unpleasant prig. But this undue *conceit* does not have to follow from having a legitimate pride and confidence in the things he does well. As long as 'good at' is not seen to be the same thing as 'better than' in anything other than comparative skill terms, it is important to let children know when and at what they have done well.

To guard against inappropriate conceit, you can again apply the distinction between the *deed* and the *person*. You can be impressed by what your child can do; but it should not make you value him as an individual any more or less. As soon as you begin to confuse the two, you enter dangerous territory. If he begins to brag about his achievements, it might be because this has become the only means by which he can value himself.

You should be able to encourage a legitimate pride without this developing into conceit if you:
- value your child for who he is, and praise him for what he has done

- ensure that you value a variety of skills so that your child learns tolerance
- teach that 'good at' means 'different from', not 'better than'.

Praise is undoubtedly important to a child's sense of value and worth; but be careful how you give it. Remember: you are generally on safe ground if you:

- appreciate rather than approve
- describe and praise the deed rather than the person
- praise the process, in other words the effort and improvement, rather than the product.

Praise and you
- Ask for it if you want to hear it.
- Tell yourself, and believe it, if you think you did something well.
- Reward yourself.
- The more you show you appreciate others, the more likely they are to show that they appreciate you.
- If someone praises you, accept it and hold on to it. Don't squirm or hand it back, saying you don't deserve it, or 'it was nothing'. Just say '*Thank you.*'

Peace

Children just as much as anyone else need time and space to relax and wind down, a time to feel at rest and at ease with themselves. Everyone has his own way of unwinding. Some people need to flop in front of the television for a while. Some need to be alone, to 'fiddle about' aimlessly –

with their toys, or in the garden. Some like to kick a ball, or bury themselves in the newspaper, or soak in a bath. Others like to sit with a cup of tea, or have a beer at the bar. Whatever it is, we all need it. We don't always get it, or take it; but which particular thing we choose to do to unwind says something important about who we are. Being quiet during these times gives us a chance to let our thoughts roam. It is a time to reflect and, most important, to find out what is inside us and to learn to be happy with ourselves.

Peace means:
- the chance to wind down and relax, or even escape
- calm
- quiet togetherness
- being alone
- rest
- sleep
- silence
- the absence of arguments and tension

We do not have to be alone to experience this regenerating peace. We can be quiet with others there, too. We need opportunities to realise that relationships can exist without words, that we can still feel togetherness without action and conversation; in other words, that silence as communion can be a form of communication and that someone's company is enough to make you feel at ease. One of the limitations of the 'quality time' that working parents often aim to give their children when they get home is that it tends to be action-packed. There will be a lot of talk. There may be games. The child may be asked to describe her day when her mind has wandered a long way away from earlier events. The time given to the child is too contrived. It pays no attention to her mood and does not acknowledge the value of quiet togetherness and spontaneity. There is too much 'ought' about the time spent together and not enough 'want', with the child being booked in to the parents' day and expected to meet their expectations rather than the other way around.

If the atmosphere at home is so emotionally charged and difficult – or just busy and crowded – that it cannot readily offer restful space, perhaps a relative, friend or neighbour could provide the bolt hole instead.

Action plan
- Discover your child's mechanisms for winding down.
- Encourage her to do it.
- Respect her need for her own space, even if it is not in your home.
- Encourage quiet togetherness – e.g., watch TV together, give time for morning cuddles in bed if she is young enough, or sit with her silently stroking her face as she goes to sleep.

Peace and you
You need to give yourself peaceful time in order to reflect, to regain the strength to cope and to reassure yourself that you can be content with your own company – that you can be your own friend.

If you need to be busy all the time, ask yourself why, and make yourself sit, quietly and alone, and see how it makes you feel and what you get from it.

Your action plan

- Identify your own mechanisms for winding down.
- Try to spend fifteen minutes every day 'with your feet up', at rest, however you like to do it.
- Try to have some quiet togetherness with those who are close to you.

Play

Through play, children:

- find out who they are
- discover what they can do
- realise they can manage on their own

Finding out who they are: developing self-esteem

It would be hard to overemphasise the importance of play in children's development and, in particular, the development of their self-esteem. Play is, and should be, about choices. As children play, they make many choices. They have to choose what to play. They have to choose where to play. They may be able to choose who to play with. If they are painting or colouring, they have to choose what to draw, and which colour to do it in. If they are playing imaginatively, with others or by themselves, they have to choose the story-line, which characters are to be in the story and, most importantly, who they are going to be. If they are playing ball with friends, they have to choose the rules that will apply. If they are dressing up, they have to choose what to put on. All of these choices help to build up a picture of themselves – what they like to do, who they like to be with – and gives them a sense of being in control of their lives.

Making choices in the context of play makes the experience of choosing easy and 'safe'. They are safe because there is no right or wrong decision. 'Make-believe', cutting paper, arranging bricks or squishing modelling material can take any form. Nothing hangs on it. Identity and confidence can develop, unrestrained by fear of mistake and failure. As children get older, and their identity is better established, they are more able to cope with the challenge of play which is structured and governed by rules – which has winners and losers. Play with few or no choices, on the other hand – the kind of play which is tightly managed by an adult – can teach certain things. But what it does not provide is opportunities to reveal, without fear or failure, what it is which makes you 'you'.

Discovering what they can do: developing self-confidence
Play develops many skills – physical, social and intellectual. Imaginative play helps to develop language (because children chatter as they invent) and the ability to create stories. It also helps with social skills, teaching how to approach and get on with others, compromise or negotiate. Running and climbing develops physical coordination. Being in control of their own bodies, and being strong and vigorous, is often children's first experience of real pride and achievement. Physical activity also promotes a general fitness that will not only have life-long benefits but will also contribute to stamina and competence in a wide range of tasks. Play helps children to develop problem-solving and planning skills that are part of life. Experiencing failures outside the real world where it does not matter helps them to manage and cope with failure when they do have to account for it. Playing with others introduces children to

different ideas, hobbies and ways of thinking which enriches their experience and gives them a wider range of resources on which to draw.

Realising they can manage on their own: developing self-reliance

Children need opportunities to play and experiment free from adult supervision and scrutiny; and they need this more the older they get. If we hover over them, ready to solve any little problem that may arise, they cannot learn to cope on their own. As children get older they need – in the safety of a group – to venture further afield and explore the world outside their home. It may be comfortable for us to have our children safely indoors watching TV, or travelling somewhere with us; but such protection may not be in their long-term best interests. Children also need to learn to amuse themselves: to become more self-directed, to discover constructive solutions to boredom and be assured that they can have a sense of being, purpose and contentment without the presence of others.

Sharing their play

While children need the chance to explore their experiences and feelings, alone and separate from the adult's critical eye, there are times when a child needs you to join in, provided that you don't then take it over. Your child's play may seem daft, and you will almost certainly feel daft. But you are needed not only to provide the role that he is examining but also so that he may validate himself because you *accept* his play which is *his* creation. It is essential that parents give children opportunities for spontaneous play, particularly for imaginative play, and show an interest in what their children play. Children's play must never be belittled, or their fantasy shattered. When you play with your child, he will believe that you play the game with him because you enjoy and love him so much. How can you make sure that you do not direct and interfere with his play?

Don't undermine your child by capping or improving his ideas. Adult ideas will invariably be more sophisticated than a child's. By improving your child's ideas you don't teach him how to do it better next time – only that his ideas and he himself fall short and are not good enough. If you want to suggest options to extend his thinking, keep them for next time and offer them before the play starts.

Don't devalue aimless play. Again, the shape it eventually takes (and it almost certainly will take on a shape) is a measure of the child's creative abilities and his growing sense of identity – who he is and what he likes and does not like. Force him to do something which *you* recognise as purposeful and you are not only in danger of imposing your view of what is 'appropriate' play, but also transmitting that you do not trust his choice or approve of what he does to 'be himself'. This could be interpreted as not approving of who he is.

Some children find it difficult to play. They need some help to have and be confident about ideas, and they need to learn how to be creative and develop story-lines. If you have a child who seems to freeze up when asked to 'play something', perhaps you could play with him and carefully guide him through a range of possibilities. This may be difficult for you. Many adults feel desperately uncomfortable with childlike fantasy. But children are not necessarily aware of this discomfort. You could start by involving them in the normal, daily things that you do and then acting these out with their cuddly toys. Sitting down with paper and crayons and drawing together is another easy way into the child's world.

Imaginative play

Imaginative play is a child's opportunity for the most individualised creativity totally free from the frustrations and constrictions of undeveloped skills. It frees the mind. Fantasy allows endless possibilities. Play, therefore, also develops mental agility and flexibility. In imaginative play, there are no ground rules that have been set by anyone else either of a structured, game-oriented type or of a physical nature (for example, hold the pencil this way, don't mess up the colours in the paintbox, don't let it drop on the floor). If the activity exists in the child's imagination, nothing can go wrong. They are in a world beyond criticism and beyond practical mishap where they are not only safe but also in control. If you join in with them, they not only control the fantasy but it also enables them, in a sense, to control you. We are back again to the all-important dimension of power in the adult–child relationship. Children do feel acutely their lack of power compared with adults. If they feel that power is abused, they will try and get their own back by developing all sorts of manipulative strategies. Give them plenty of chances to be on the other side of the fence and wield the power in play and fantasy, as well as in real choices about their life, and the need to manipulate and get their own back – to play power back at you – will diminish.

Play as therapy

Entering children's play and giving them the opportunity to control you either by active role reversal or just by letting them take charge of the events of the fantasy/drama may well release resentment. It should not now need to be said that, when you enter that fantasy, you must not start to direct it. Play along with it, yes. Shape it and develop the events in your allocated role, yes. There is a big difference between the statement *'Let's do it this way'* and *'How do you think it would work if we did it this way?'* But if you take it over, or if you undermine it by transferring in and out of the make-believe to your real world to do forgotten jobs, thereby indicating that you don't take it seriously and respect their needs, the time you have spent with them may well have been wasted.

Play also gives children a chance to act out situations which they soon have to face, which they are currently going through, or which they have recently been through, in order to sort things out – to become more familiar and comfortable with changes and perhaps to increase their understanding, and thereby their sense of security. They may want, and need, to play the same things over and over again. The same benefit can be gained from reading stories about events that can be stressful. When children are going into hospital or starting school for the first time, they will often become almost obsessed with books describing what is likely to happen, or telling a story around the life change, wanting to have them read to them repeatedly. At times of change and stress, children should have relevant books or play materials close by to look at and exploit if they feel the need.

Play is also a useful tool for parents to use to relieve both their own and their child's anxiety by replaying something that has happened. It seems to be particularly useful to the child for the parent or carer to change places with them –

with the adult being the naughty child, for example, making the incident quite ridiculous and turning it into the safe arena of farce. Humour can heal a great deal. For example, if you play a 'let's pretend' game about going out shopping, you can include fights over buying sweets, arguments over how many packets of biscuits you will get, and sulks about having to go out in the first place. Role reversal can also be used effectively when you think your child feels resentful about being overpowered. Another technique is to use dolls or soft toys to take on different characters, to replay something that happened in the family or at school – being told off, for example.

All changes are stressful, particularly those which overturn established routines. This is as true for children as it is for us. We can talk through our anxieties with our friends, but young children cannot. We can explore our relationships and difficulties through reading novels or going to the cinema. Young children cannot. Play is the only route for them to work through their insecurities and to explore the possibilities. Art and music, the other expressive outlets, may help to release tensions, anger or other emotions, but they cannot be as effective as play in working out solutions and strategies for the problems which children encounter in their world.

Play and television

Watching television is a form of leisure, but it is not play. It can provide ideas to be used in play (craft ideas or scenarios for 'let's pretend') and it can be used to wind down and relax, but it would be a mistake to say that television is, or offers the same kind of experience as, quality play.

Leisure is normally understood as free time, time at your own disposal to do what you like with. *Play*, according to the dictionary, is 'moving about in a lively manner', 'amusing oneself', 'pretending for fun', or 'being involved in a game'. Broadcast television, as distinct from computer or video games displayed on a screen, does not qualify under any of these definitions.

If choices are an important part of *quality play* (that is, play which enhances the self and offers scope for experiment and personal, including language, development), television certainly cannot qualify. We know that young children are believed to have poorer language skills when starting school than hitherto, and television is thought to contribute to this. Indeed some psychologists now consider television to be unsuitable for children under two years old. For older children, what choices, apart from changing the channel, or pressing the on/off button, does it offer? Television can inform; television can educate; television can offer a variety of models of relationships for children to observe. Sitcoms or drama on television can extend children's concepts of experience and fiction, and give them insights into relationships and situations that might be troubling them personally. But television cannot build on or manifest a child's inner resources for coping, develop her powers of intuition, or deepen her sense of herself as profoundly as does the 'hands-on' experience of play.

Quality play involves:
- choices
- imagination
- other people, real or created
- experimentation

It encourages creativity, curiosity, confidence, concentration, cooperation and physical coordination. So: *make space* for them to play in; *make time* to play with them; and make sure that some of this time is spent in *make-believe*.

What can they play?

Unstructured or 'free' play

Creative play is pre-social play which children can do on their own before they are able to play cooperatively or sustain complex story-lines. (For example, painting, using soft modelling materials, drawing, cutting and sticking.) Creative play develops manipulative skills, ideas, encourages experimentation, develops confidence in making choices, and offers a channel for children to explore themselves and their talents.

Imaginative play encourages inventiveness, putting ideas into words, interpersonal and problem-solving skills.

Physical play develops strength and coordination, both of which are needed for early experiences of competence.

Structured play: rule-governed and 'directional'

Rule-governed play (for example, team sports or board or card games) develops notions of 'fairness' and cooperation in all players if everyone abides by the rules.

'Directional' play is non-competitive (for example, jigsaws and craft skills). It encourages 'stickability', or task commitment – the ability to stay with a task or activity until it is completed.

Play and you

Play and enjoy yourself so you feel happy and fulfilled and not resentful. If you enjoy doing a number of different things, your child will learn not only how to use his own time constructively, but also that you like to play, and that you have needs too, which are part of your boundaries and which have to be respected.

*T*RUST, *T*OUCH, *T*IME, *T*ALK

Trust

A fundamental and mutual trust is created between mother and infant at birth. It is almost imprinted, since the notion of trust implies an expectation and can therefore only really develop after some experiences over time (however short) which establish that expectation. At the moment of birth, however, the infant must trust that the mother will care and provide for her, and the mother trusts, on her part, that the infant will love and need her. If the mother does not believe that that will be the case, then why should she bother to take on the responsibility of rearing the child? It is the infinite, or at least undefined, degree of need for care and nurture which both triggers the instinct to care and love in the mother (in most instances) yet also can terrify her so much that she withdraws into a depression in order to hold on to her self.

So, from the very beginning, an unspoken and reciprocated simple trust exists. Later, any failure to trust your growing child will equate to putting him down. Growing up involves facing new things – situations and experiences – at a rate that most adults would find enormously stressful. It takes great courage to embark on something new, and self-belief is vital to meet challenges with confidence. Imagine the hurt and the blow to your pride if the person you most rely on to help you judge your capabilities assumes that you are unlikely to manage or achieve something – often before you have even really tried.

Trust your child . . .
- Trust your child's competence – his ability to achieve something. *'Shall I help you?'* while seeming supportive, in fact sends a message that you don't think he is going to manage. *'Call me if you need me'* is better.
- Trust his ability to complete something. Always put the past behind. Let him start each new venture or attempt with a clean sheet of expectations.
- Trust his judgement.
- Trust his sense of responsibility.
- Trust, and praise, his ideas.

. . . and don't abuse your child's trust in you.

Trust and you
- Trust your ability to be a 'positive parent'.
- Trust that your child needs and wants *you* more than he wants anyone else.
- Trust the relationship you have with your child, which will have its natural ups and downs. Try not to test out his love, curry favour, or to interpret his disappointments as a rejection of you. Parents have to be parents first, and friends second.

Touch

Never withdraw your body; give your child somewhere safe to hide

For some reason, we in Western societies seem to have lost the habit of touching each other. We are very happy to spend hours fondling our pets and really enjoy the pleasure they seem to get from it. We enjoy it too, relishing their soft fur. Indeed, stroking them has a physical, calming effect on us with such a powerful impact on our biological functions that animals are often used therapeutically to help people recover from surgery and stress-related illnesses. Despite this, we seem to be totally insensitive to the need of our fellow human beings, adults and children, for the warmth, reassurance and pure physical pleasure that comes from touching, stroking and caressing. This is in contrast to Eastern cultures, in which the therapeutic value of touch and massage has been acknowledged for centuries. It is certainly not considered appropriate for mature adults, outside a growing romantic relationship, to walk about with their arms round each other or hold hands. It is even becoming less common for people to touch by the more formal method of shaking hands. Why?

Quite simply, we are getting out of the habit of touching, and to touch 'feels' like an increasingly strange and difficult thing to do. But there may be more to it than that. Touching is also an important expression of giving, and a sign of equality and empathy (hence the contrived political handshake and arm squeeze); and fewer people today seem to be able to give – to feel equal and sufficiently confident to make that physical statement of giving.

A child who is not touched is a child who will feel

ignored, ashamed, unworthy of attention, inferior and misunderstood. In short, that child will feel lost, alone, unsure and unhappy.

We touch our new babies, of course, when they are fed and have their nappies changed. But the mother who does more, and ties her baby to her front or props her on her hip while she walks about and does chores, is generally told off and accused of spoiling the child. When we no longer feed our children and they manage their own toileting, somehow the touching often disappears too. It is very important for *all* adults involved in caring to touch. Maternal touch is assumed to be more important than the male or paternal touch. But fathers, stepfathers and live-in boyfriends all need to think about the child's need to be accepted and approved by them. Of course, we need to be aware of the important cultural, gender and legal differences between appropriate and inappropriate touching. This appeal to recognise a child's need for physical affection should not be interpreted as an invitation to engage in inappropriate or abusive behaviour. But anyone who has a sufficiently close and regular relationship with a child, such that the child begins to assess and understand herself through that relationship, must acknowledge the child's need to know that she is loved and believed in as can be expressed so spontaneously through appropriate touch.

Touch has a language of its own. It can say so much, in so many different ways, and it need take only a split second. It can be a full embrace. It can be an arm around the shoulders. It can ask for nothing in return, or it can demand something back, an equal response or at least an acknowledgement that the hidden message has been received.

It is a mistake just to touch your child when *you* need it; for example, when you need reassurance, to feel loved, or to calm down after a stressful experience. To touch only at these times comes close to treating children like pets. Of course, children can give us enormous consolation when we are upset. Their love replenishes us when we are down. But what about when *they* are down? What about *their* need for reassurance and consolation? If they come to us for a cuddle when *they* feel they need it, do we accept it even if it is not desperately convenient? Or do we put the thing we are busy with first? It can be very damaging to their pride, and therefore a potential threat to your relationship, to reject spontaneous expressions of affection especially if you are still angry about something they have done. Beneath their gesture will lie not only very complex emotions but also a desperate need to love you and to be loved by you. The touch they want to give you is saying something far too complex for them to express in words. It will say: *'I need you. I am sorry. Please tell me, by accepting my touch, that you still want me even though my behaviour has been awful.'* It would be even better if we could get in first, reading the signs in advance that what they really need is understanding and reassurance.

Touch is:
- intimate
- a statement of human equality
- a quicker form of expression than words
- less liable to misinterpretation
- an important gesture of giving
- implies mutual understanding

Kinds of touching

- One-way: giving.
- Two-way: giving and receiving.
- The habitual or ritual touch (for example, first thing in the morning, after school, returning from a friend) may seem superficial, but it is advisable to keep the practice of touching in the family so that in the difficult times, when showing affection is hard, it is easier to maintain it.
- The spontaneous touch really means something particular to the individual child – an expression of understanding of a particular experience they are having.

The vocabulary of touch

The accepting touch

- the possessive (in the best sense) touch: *'You belong to me'*
- the healing touch – after the argument
- the understanding/consoling touch
- the proud touch
- the equality touch: *'I am the same/feel the same as you'*
- the loving touch

The rejecting touch

Touch is so powerful that it is also used negatively to reject and to hurt – not just to cause pain, which it can obviously do, but to hurt feelings.

- the push away (how do *you* feel when your cuddle is pushed away? Doesn't it speak volumes?)
- the quick slap

When your cuddle/touch is brushed away: the 'snail' effect.
When a cuddle is rejected, what does it mean? It does not
mean that your child hates you for ever. It is most likely to
happen after an argument, and it means that the child has
been hurt. Like a snail whose antennae are poked, a child
will recoil and be wary of accepting the cuddle in case the
renewed trust is mistaken and the poking starts again. It is
essential that you do not, then, recoil yourself. Instead, you
should acknowledge the feelings. Don't force the cuddle,
but say that you are there and ready to receive her physical
approach when she feels ready to give it.

Touch and you
What can you do if you are still finding it difficult to be
closer physically to your child?

- Ask your partner to massage/stroke/hug you so that you
  can appreciate the benefits of this contact. Often,
  releasing the block in one part of your life can release it
  in others, too.
- If you have no partner, or your partner does not want
  to, then ask a friend, or pay for a professional
  massage.
- To make it easier, think of a touching activity to do
  with your child which is not displaying emotion. You
  could try sitting next to her while watching TV, or
  stroking her forehead as she settles to sleep.

Time
- Your child needs *you* and, sometimes, your complete
  and undivided attention.

- Don't let bad behaviour be the only way of getting attention.
- Presents are no substitute for presence.

Why is spending time with your child so important?

For children to get any sense that they are loved and wanted, you have to be prepared to spend time with them. There is no getting away from this simple truth. If you do not give them very much of your time, talking, laughing, playing, sharing things or just generally being around listening to and enjoying them, how can they possibly get any other message than that they are not worthy of your love, time and attention? How can they then progress to love themselves if they perceive that you always put yourself and others first, before them, and that they are apparently incidental to your life – even that they are a nuisance? And their need does not stop when they first go to school. They go on needing you to be interested in them and to demonstrate your love for them by spending time with them right through adolescence.

How do we know that children need so much time?

- The more you give, the more they want.
- If they do not get it, they behave badly to try and get it.

Your child will need you, love you and want you more than you can imagine. You give him his sense of belonging, his security. His need for you can seem insatiable. The more you give, it seems, the more he wants. That can be terrifying, especially if you do not feel ready to give that much; for example, if you are still exploring yourself. When children are little, they crave time and attention so badly that, if it is not given naturally and spontaneously, they will behave in whatever outrageous way they have to in order to get it. Bad behaviour is a very effective way of getting attention. If you let it be the only way to get you to take notice of them, you are unlikely to see any change, however much you discipline and punish. The cycle of poor behaviour and self-doubt can very easily turn first to self-hatred, and then to full-scale opting out of the system.

Time to do what?

Talk
Talk about your day, their day, what you are going to do, what you are seeing in the street, what you have been watching on television, what they like to do, your childhood, their relatives, their toys.

Play
Sit with them while they play, and talk to them about what they are doing.

Listen
Look at their faces when they are telling you something. If it seems important, stop what you are doing and sit down with them to hear it.

Quiet time
Sit with them while they watch TV or while they get ready for bed.

Share
Invite them to do something or go somewhere with you, to show you enjoy their company: *'Come and talk to me while I get tea ready.'*

In other words, you can:

- join them in what *they* are doing
- invite them to join you in what *you* are doing
- do something alongside them, in parallel, talking together or just being quiet together

Special time for each one

Each child in the family ideally needs to have their own special time with each of their parents. It does not have to take a vast amount of time, or have to happen every day. But each child is different, and will want to have a chance to be alone with each of you. At the root of sibling rivalry lies competition for the parents' attention. Clearly defined, individual, 'special' time given to each child in a family can lead to a marked reduction in the fights between them.

Special time can be:

- reading to them on their own at bedtime, though this is not always practical
- being there to chat while they or you have a bath, or having a bath together, if they are young enough and do not mind
- having one of them read or talk to you while you do the ironing or any DIY chores
- walking to the bus stop with them if they are older and going out somewhere

There are many different ways to give special time. It may need to be different with each child to match their needs and interests.

> What two ways can you think of to spend special time
> with each child?
>
> -
> -
> -
> -

'Quality time'

'Quality time' is an approach that has been developed to
meet the working parent's main predicament – not being
able to spend very much time at home. The idea of 'quality
time' suggests that it is not how much time we spend with
our children that matters but what we do with them when
we are around. In other words, *quality* is seen as more
important than *quantity*.

Spending quality time with our children means giving
them our whole-hearted attention, and ensuring it is
constructive, productive time spent actively doing things
with them. Quality time is therefore often seen as action-
packed time or, at least, a socially intense time. It is a very
important concept but its limitations should be understood
so that we can meet children's needs more effectively. For
example:

- Quality time does not always take account of moods
  and feelings. Instead of doing something active –
  having to play or talk – at the appointed time, a child
  may feel like being quiet with you, curling up with their
  favourite cuddly toy. *Communion*, or quiet togetherness,
  can be just as important for the relationship as active
  communication. Being sensitive to a child's moods and

needs and realising that it is just as valuable sometimes merely to be together may take some pressure off the allotted quality time.

- Having only limited time for your child can mean that you are not there at the unpredictable moment when he decides to tell you about something. When you get home, the urge to tell may have passed. To show you understand this, and to help them remember that there was something they wanted to talk about, younger children can be given a game where a particular toy is put in an agreed place where you will see it when you come in. Older children can make a note of things they want to raise, so there can be a family message pad or notice board pinned to a wall (or fridge) for general use.

  A regular session shows that you want to make space for special time but may not be sufficiently flexible to respond to your child's changing needs. There will inevitably be times when friendship problems or other anxieties make them more needy for you. It is important to show insight and sensitivity by being more available when they ask for it.

- Children can be told where appropriate that although time for actually doing things together may be limited, a parent can always be reached during the working day by telephone, e-mail or text message if there is a special problem.

  'Being there' for children does not have to mean twenty-four-hour availability but it does mean offering some flexibility on access to meet special circumstances and listening to them when they ask for it.

Time and television

Research has shown that children who watch a lot of television have significantly lower self-esteem than those who do not. This is nothing to do with what they watch, and the effect it might have on them. The low self-esteem is explained by the fact that the time spent watching is time children are *not* spending talking to their parents. They therefore get no sense of being valued, of the adults they are close to wanting to spend time with them. So rather than just nagging them to turn off the TV, next time why not try offering to do or play something with them instead?

Time and you

Try to make some time free for you to enjoy doing whatever it is you like to do. If having 'special time' alone with your partner will help you to feel wanted and valued, ask for it and organise it.

Talk (and listen!)

Talking to your child will:
- enhance the relationship
- engage his attention
- enliven him, making him feel interesting and wanted

The importance of talking to children

Talking to children helps to develop:
- their language skills – their ability to express themselves and communicate
- their sense of having a unique relationship with you
- their sense of value and self
- their social competence

Talking to children is extremely important, for two reasons. First, children need language to be able to communicate with others. It helps them express themselves and to fit in. They have to use words to show what they know – in school, for example. The more adults talk to children and babies, the easier children will find it to use and to understand words and the better they will manage their education. Second, talking is a way of showing that you care. Children who are not spoken to will feel ignored and unimportant. Talking to them, involving them, asking about what has happened to them and telling them things which have happened to you all send the message that you think they are important. Talking, therefore, is essential to creating good self-esteem.

The importance of listening to children

Listening to children helps to develop:
- their sense of being understood
- their belief that they are acknowledged and respected
- their feelings of being trusted
- their need to have somewhere safe to go to be honest
- their need to have someone who is there for them

Listening to children involves more than hearing their words. We must also 'hear' their actions. What children do can speak volumes about what is happening inside their heads. Words are not the only currency of communication.

Beware too much talk, and using words as tools of power and control

Adults can use words to:
- entangle, through using logic and reason which is too sophisticated and difficult for children to understand

- entrap, tripping children up, as in a courtroom, through clever questions
- engulf, smother and swamp children's feelings. When children are pre-verbal, they feel, they perceive. When words develop, they can be used to conceal

Quality talk

'Quality talk' is talking to someone and opening up the conversation so that it becomes two-way, with each person listening to and hearing the other. When we talk to our children, we must make sure we say things which start a conversation, which encourage them to join in. This is very different from 'talking at' someone, when we direct comments or questions but seem uninterested in the other person's reactions. The two approaches can be illustrated thus:

Talk to $\rightarrow$ Message listened to $\rightarrow$ Answer/ Respond $\rightarrow$ An opening/ expanding exchange

Talk at $\rightarrow$ Message bounces off $\rightarrow$ Incident ignored $\rightarrow$ A closed-off exchange

'Talking at' will include asking children a question, and then answering it for them. For example, *'What would you like to drink? I know, milk's your favourite at the moment, so I'll get you that.'*

What can you talk about?

Anything. Babies are happy with just the sound of our voices, so when children are very small we can simply describe whatever it is we are doing or the cars or trees that we are passing. Later, we can talk about what we have done during the day, what we have read in a magazine, or what we have seen on television. We can ask about their day, what they enjoyed, who they talked to. Later still, when some of those questions may be rejected as prying, if we focus on the things which interest them we can try to keep the lines of communication open.

Talk and you

If you want someone to talk to you, start the conversation and ask for it!

EMPATH*ISE*, SYMPATH*ISE*, APOLOG*ISE*, COMPROM*ISE*

Empath*ise*

'My mum doesn't understand me!'

Teenagers often feel misunderstood. Although they would probably prefer to be understood by their parents, if they are not, they will not be alone in the world – most will have a sizeable group of friends who will be on the same wavelength and with whom they identify. In fact, adolescents typically group to boost their confidence and sense of identity and belonging while they come to terms with the idea of growing away from their parents.

Young children do not have that luxury. A child who feels misunderstood will also feel very much alone. She cannot consult her friends in playgroup or infant school, asking if they feel the same way. The very thought of such a discussion is ludicrous. Even if such things were discussed, most children would find it well nigh impossible to put such intangible and complicated feelings and experiences into words.

Most people who live closely together, especially parents and children, develop an intuitive sense about each other. When babies are small and cannot talk, we rely totally on intuition to understand how they are feeling – why they are crying. It starts off as guesswork, but we gradually build an understanding of our child's patterns and personality. It is often easier said than done. You can feel extremely stupid taking your nearly new baby to the doctor over something that worries you and being unable to answer their question, 'Is she normally like this?' In reality, you still have not got a clue what is normal. Every day they seem to be different. Even when we do feel more in touch, we start by interpreting their cries and communications in terms of physiological needs – hunger, too hot or too cold, tummy pain – rather than emotional feelings. We tend not to consider that the helpless infant can also feel bored, isolated, frightened, angry or in desperate need of the security of a cuddle.

The normal range of physiological needs do, in fact, tell us something about individuals. We can learn that our children have their own individual body rhythms. For example, one might like to eat most at midday, while another might feel most hungry after school. One might never seem to feel the cold, while another might need to wear many layers even in summer. Of course, children have to learn to adjust and fit into a family routine. But this need not involve them losing their identity if their individual patterns are understood and acknowledged.

Apart from our basic physiological blueprint, it is our 'finer' feelings, or the lack of them, which make us who we are and which give us our sense of self. That certain things frustrate us, make us happy, interest us, upset us or hurt us makes us who we are. We could not be 'us' if we did not feel and react in this particular way to those particular things. If, as parents, we are able to recognise these 'particularities', and therefore not only to understand where our children are coming from but also to show some respect for how they see their world, we will be able to empathise with them. Empathy means being able to know, or to have a good guess, how they might be feeling about something and that it is real for them. You do not have to agree with their view. But if you can at least appreciate *their* dilemma, at *their* level, they will not feel the pain of isolation or the puzzlement and grief of losing your support. We can only empathise with someone if we have some personal experience of our own which lets us know what it means to, for example, lose a pet (bereavement) or come last in a race (failure and humiliation). Either we have had similar experiences or we have had feelings close enough to allow us to enter imaginatively into someone else's emotions. Someone who has never experienced such feelings or who is completely out of touch with their own emotions, cannot empathise, they can only sympathise.

Understanding a child should not be especially difficult. It rarely involves more than understanding ourselves and acknowledging how we felt in the past. However, this can be tricky; many of us bury our own feelings so deep that it is hard or painful to get back in touch with them though it will enrich our lives if we can. Getting close to our children can be a doubly rewarding experience if we can also get back in touch with ourselves – even if it does force us to reflect on some uncomfortable things. You will need to:

- talk to your child
- listen to what she says about her feelings
- hear what her actions say about her wishes, pleasures and pains
- be open and honest with yourself and with her; this will help to release your feelings

Openness and honesty go hand in hand with empathy.

What does empathy mean in practice?

'When my ten-year-old son left his swimming things at home on swimming day for the second week running, and the third time that term, I was as mad as anything. But I knew that he hadn't done it on purpose. I realised that there was no point in giving him a hard time, because it would make no difference to whether he forgot them another week. I realised how awful it must have been for him, sitting out again and feeling so stupid. When he got home I said, "It must have been so awful for you, feeling so embarrassed and stupid in front of the teacher and the whole class." "You're right," he replied. He never forgot them again.'

We often throw out questions that imply that we are accusing our children of something, such as:

- *'Why do you insist on wearing those ludicrous clothes?'*
- *'Why do you spend all day in front of the television?'*
- *'Why do you always hit your sister?'*
- *'Why must you always get so dirty?'*
- *'Why are you such a fidget?'*

Instead, we can try seeing it from their point of view. We can guess at their answer, and voice it for them, showing that we are attempting to understand them. We can then rephrase our questions so they become more like statements:

- *'That outfit is obviously a favourite. Is that what everyone's wearing now? Can't say I go for it!'*
- *'I think you must be feeling bored.'*
- *'I realise that you sometimes feel angry at your sister, but hitting her isn't the way to show it.'*
- *'You get so carried away with your games, you don't think of my pile of washing, do you?'*
- *'It seems hard for you to sit still at the table for the whole meal. I used to feel wriggly, too.'*

Empathy is practical

A parent who can show that she understands what her child is feeling will be more successful at getting him to do things he does not, initially, want to. He will not feel put down or put upon. He will not feel ignored. He will not feel resentful. Empathy is the best way to demonstrate to your child not only that you can be on the same wavelength as him, but also that you are still there for him . . . *and that you are on his side.*

Empathy and you

Ask your children and your partner to see things from your point of view. Either ask them to listen, and tell them what it is, or invite them to imagine what your reasons might be. Invite them also to consider how you might feel about something that has happened or that they have done.

Sympath*ise*

To sympathise means to share what someone is feeling. Sympathy is different from empathy. While empathy with a child involves *understanding* and getting close to what an experience means for them, sympathy just requires us to exercise compassion and commiseration that tells them it is OK to be feeling the way they do – their feelings are legitimate.

Sometimes we fail to give sympathy because we hate our children to be sad, disappointed or hurt. We want to pretend that they are really all right and we press them to feel better. If we have been responsible for their disappointment, we may feel guilty, so there is even more reason to want them to 'get over it' quickly. The assumption is that if we ask or tell them to stop feeling, this will influence the matter. It won't. Whatever reasons we may offer to help disperse the feelings, they won't want to hear them. They only feel their disappointment, sadness or pain and are aware that we seem not to appreciate the scale of what they feel. If we do not at least accept their feelings, and say something like, *'That's a big hurt, isn't it?'* the message children receive will be *'My mother expects me to be more reasonable and mature than I can be.'*

Apolog*ise*

An apology is a sign of strength, not weakness
Many people believe that if they apologise to a child, they weaken themselves and the rules they are trying to keep. They also believe it will make the child think their behaviour was OK after all. It is important to realise that this need not be so.

You can apologise for what *you* did, how you responded to a child's behaviour, without condoning or accepting what *the child* did. This distinction can be important.

Apologising in this way makes it clear that you are not weakening the rules. It will not be a sign of weakness. It will not be the start of a behavioural slippery slope down towards chaos. It will not undermine your authority – your ability to make the rules or to expect compliance. It *will* set a good example and encourage your child to be open and apologise when he has done wrong.

Apologising demonstrates:
- equality in terms of human rights
- empathy for what you might have done to their feelings
- respect for their right to be treated fairly

Apologising is similar to praise. If you are feeling vulnerable and playing power, and trying to keep a position of safe distance and superiority, it is something you do not do. If, on the other hand, you feel strong and not threatened, you will not feel you lose anything important by doing it.

Apologising teaches that:
- you can admit error without loss of face
- your self-esteem is strong enough to be left intact
- you are prepared to take responsibility
- everyone makes mistakes sometimes
- you, and your child, can survive mistakes

Admitting error and taking responsibility
Apologising involves taking responsibility for your behaviour and accepting that you did something wrong which

you regret. It also means that you take responsibility (and at the same time take it away from the child) for the sequence of events linked to your regretted reaction – which is frequently part of a downward spiral of increasingly unpleasant and unseemly behaviour which the child will be feeling very uncomfortable about.

If you do not formally accept responsibility for your behaviour, and yet you none the less feel bad about what you did or what has happened, you might feel tempted to dump your bad feelings on someone else. You might make someone else responsible for it by laying the blame elsewhere. People frequently blame others nearby for things which are either nobody's fault, or are really their own fault. When you are passing the responsibility over to children, and blaming them, this is usually extremely unfair. You will make them feel guilty and resentful.

If you find that you frequently blame others for your mistakes, or for your intolerance or bad temper (*'If you had not got me looking for your toy, then I wouldn't have burnt the saucepan!' 'If you had not kept on nagging me about that trip to the shops, I wouldn't have lost my temper with you over this!'*), think carefully about why you seem to feel unwilling to take responsibility for your own behaviour. It might be because you feel pretty bad about yourself. It might be because you cannot tolerate failure or anything less than perfection. Instead of laying blame on others, each time you feel yourself about to do it, just say, *'I'm sorry for what I did'* or *'Wasn't that silly of me!'* or even something quite neutral such as, *'I wish that had not happened'*, and see what effect it has on you and your family. It probably will not be so difficult to carry the responsibility. What, after all, can really happen to you if you do 'own up'? No one is there to punish you except yourself. And the other members of the family will feel respect for you rather than resentment. If you show that it is OK to go public about your mistakes and apologise for them, you will encourage others in your family to do the same.

Surviving mistakes

Showing that you have the strength to admit to, and survive, mistakes encourages children to have the same strength in their dealings with others outside the family. More important, perhaps, is the demonstration that the relationship can survive errors. You can approach them again, with your olive branch, to make amends, and you give them the option to do the same in return. Apologising also offers the chance to both give and experience forgiveness. If children grow up with the experience of apology and forgiveness within the family, and with an appropriate sense of proportion about the sometimes ridiculous positions we get ourselves into, they will be far better able to negotiate their way through the minefield of relationships in later life.

Different ways of apologising

Different ways of saying sorry include:
- saying it in words
- doing something for your child
- buying something for your child

In words

> *'I'm sorry that I got back later than I said I would.'*
> *'I feel awful that I shouted at you this morning.'*
> *'I wish I hadn't yelled just then. I feel terrible about it.'*

'You did a very naughty thing but I should never have been so horrid to you.'

'I feel horrible inside because I was so horrid to you.'

'I was very silly to get so upset about your messy room.'

Doing something

Doing something special with and for your child can be more powerful than just saying sorry. It shows that you really mean it. It is a way of repaying them, of evening it out. You might give them their favourite food for tea, read an extra long story at bedtime, or sit and play with them. If saying sorry is hard for you, you do not have to say why you are being extra nice. They will just feel happier because you are giving them special attention, and the resentment will be easier to forget.

However, we cannot do this too often. Too many swings of behaviour, from nasty to very nice without any warning or explanation, are very puzzling and unsettling. It is much better to get used to saying sorry so that our children can understand and predict our behaviour.

Buying something

Giving children time and attention almost always means more to them than buying them something, but *little* surprises given alongside a verbal apology shows that you have given thought to what happened and feel genuine remorse.

Beware apologising too much

There are dangers in apologising too much. The problem lies not with the apology itself, but with the reason for the frequency. If you apologise a lot, you could be conveying uncertainty and guilt. If you consider that you might be doing it too much, it will be worthwhile asking whether you feel uncertain and, if so, why. Children need to feel they can rely on you, the parent. They want you to know your mind. They want you to be sure about what you are doing. They need you to be their rock, a safe and secure place to tether themselves, giving them scope to wander in safety, knowing precisely where you will be and what attitude you will have when they come back. They rely on you for sound guidance. If you wander, too, they will not like it. Rather than apologise when you are not sure whether you have done the right thing, it might be better sometimes to *feel* sorry about something but to stay quiet. How can you decide when is the right time to say nothing? This could relate to how much you perceive your child's feelings have been hurt by the action you regret; and by your own judgement about how much is too much.

What happens if you do not apologise?

If someone is clearly in the wrong, and does not apologise for their behaviour, it can cause enormous resentment. Almost certainly, every adult will have some incident from their own childhood etched on their memory when they felt unfairly treated. Children have an acute sense of fairness. They will be fair to you and to others if you are fair to them. Resentment grows and eats away at the good feelings. It is also like a barrier. It grows in thickness and height, gradually cutting off the resentful child from the object of resentment who is causing them distress.

Apologies and you

- If you want to hear them, you need to give them.
- Apologies make you feel better about yourself. They are a statement of honesty and wipe the slate clean.
- If they are given, make sure you accept them.

Compromise

A compromise, like an apology, is often seen as weakness, 'giving in' and the start of a drift towards anarchy. Too often we feel that our authority will be undermined if we do not stick to what we first demand, if we do not rigorously enforce the rules, come what may. But in truth, a compromise shows respect and understanding for the other person's wishes, activities and feelings.

Compromise is:
- a process of giving and taking
- a sign of strength, not weakness
- a win–win solution

Not to listen and respond fairly to our children's reasonable complaints, or to what they say they want, is likely to make them resentful and angry. We will end up with less authority in their eyes, and less respect from them. Great damage can be done to the relationship in the name of 'parental authority' when parents dig in their heels regardless of the genuine importance of an issue.

Compromise is not the same thing as negotiation
Negotiation implies the right to say 'no' and to walk away from agreeing to something.

Compromise involves giving and taking. Some kind of deal is assumed. The only point at issue is what form it will take – who will give way on what. It involves looking at the separate and common interests and seeing if there is a way for each person to get some, most, or all of what they want.

If a compromise is to be a win–win solution and not a

win–lose one, it follows that what you are prepared to give is not going to be very important to you – that it does not cost you too much.

For example, provided you get the shopping done that morning (non-negotiable), you do not mind whether you do it early or late (area of compromise). Your child has two favourite morning TV programmes, one early and one late. He wants to watch both. But he cannot. There is not the time to get the shopping done in between them. You are prepared to time your shopping so he can watch one, the one he likes best, but not to put it off until the afternoon so he can watch both.

Compromise is not the same thing as surrender

It is important not to confuse compromising with surrendering. Compromise does not mean that *any* concession will do.

For example, in the above situation, it might happen that your child refuses to choose one of the programmes and throws a tantrum. If you then agree, after all, to shop in the afternoon, but say that in return he will have to put away all his toys before bedtime, you would be climbing down. The fact that he agrees to do something else in return does not make it a win–win compromise.

How to seek a compromise

Some issues are negotiable; some are not. Those issues that are non-negotiable should be identified very clearly from the start with the statement, *'There is no room for negotiation on this. It has to be.'* Where there is room for compromise, it often develops naturally when everybody's separate and common interests are explored. If you do not bother to ask why your child wants something to happen differently, or to explain why you need something to happen a particular way, you will never get to common ground, the territory of compromise.

The language you use to reach a compromise can be important.

Don't say: *'I will do this if you will do that.'*
Do say: *'If we do it this way, we can both get what we want.'*

The first option can be seen as manipulative and conditional. This may come back at you later as your child learns the tactics of manipulation. It is better to state that there seems to be a solution in the middle that meets both of your needs.

The dangers in compromising too much

Too much compromise can teach a child to manipulate. The arguments used have got to be relevant. If you justify your demands with layers of arguments, you teach them to try reason after reason. Although it is good for children to be able to reason and muster a good case, they also need to be able to accept when no means no, to learn how to live with the disappointment of not getting their way, and to accept that they cannot always control events.

6

Words Matter:

SO LET'S CHANGE THE SCRIPT! . . . AND TURN THE 'PUT-DOWNS' INTO 'PUFF-UPS'

WHAT IS A 'PUT-DOWN'?

A put-down is an unnecessarily negative statement which has the effect of making the recipient feel less good about themselves, of damaging their self-respect and belief in themselves and their competence. It is a comment that says something derogatory about who someone is or about what they can do. It is therefore something that addresses either *personality* or *capability*.

Put-downs:
- humiliate
- lower dignity
- damage self-respect
- make someone feel small or unimportant
- make someone feel incompetent
- burst the bubble of confidence
- give someone bad feelings about themselves

Put-downs inevitably create some distance between the giver and the receiver, both because the person on the receiving end is bound to recoil at the sense of insult and humiliation, and because the person who utters the offending comment establishes the distance in the very act of putting himself or herself in judgement over the other.

A put-down is therefore also a 'push-away'. It is a verbal assault. Put-downs can seriously damage relationships and individuals, especially if they are frequent. They can cause resentment and create distance and resistance. When the child grows up, his poor self-image and lack of trust can affect all his subsequent relationships. Someone who is put down a lot will also be less likely to stand up for others because, far from empathising and feeling the same hurt or humiliation, they are more likely to relish the fact that someone else is in the firing line for a change.

Yet put-downs are not always delivered with evil intent. They can become almost involuntary – said without thinking – because we get into set ways of saying things and rarely think about their impact. Our words can become almost predetermined, as if they were scripted in a play.

If we are to establish a good and healthy relationship with our children and convey to them that we like them and are comfortable with them, it is clear that we have to reduce the number of reprimands we use which undermine them. Deciding to change the script, and write the put-down out of it, does not mean that we can never tell children off. It does mean that we comment on their behaviour in ways that do not damage their self-respect and make them doubt our commitment to them.

Why are children so vulnerable to put-downs?

Deep down, most of us are quite insecure and it is very easy to believe the worst of what someone says about us. Children have fewer opportunities than adults to meet people outside the home who will give them independent feedback about how likeable they are. What is said to them at home, then, will have a significant impact, especially as it will be said by the people they love most in the world. It will need at least three puff-ups to cancel out the damage of one serious put-down.

WHAT IS A 'PUFF-UP'?

A puff-up is the opposite of a put-down. Instead of deflating someone's ego, it is a descriptive or affirmative comment which builds up someone's view of themselves and makes them feel good about themselves and what they can do. It will allow their ego to swell a little, to puff up with pride, and give them a warm glow of approval and achievement.

Many people dislike the idea of giving a little boost to their child's ego. It smacks of flattery. They think it might make their child big-headed. However, provided a child realises that his particular abilities do not make him better as a person than others less talented, there is every reason to let him know what he is good at. Unpleasant bigheadedness can be avoided as long as 'good at' is not seen to be the same thing as 'better than' in anything other than comparative skill terms.

To guard against inappropriate conceit while encouraging a legitimate pride, we can apply the distinction between the deed and the person that was raised earlier in the section on 'Praise' (page 102).

- Value them for who they are, and praise them for what they have done.
- Ensure that we value a variety of skills so that children learn tolerance.
- Teach that 'good at' means 'different from', not 'better than'.

Within this framework, children should be able to manage a more competitive environment which stimulates and challenges, and offers the incentive to achieve and improve. Contrary to widespread popular belief, the absence of challenge and competition does not necessarily make children feel happy and unthreatened. Lack of challenge can damage self-esteem just as effectively as too much of the wrong kind of challenge.

HOW TO CHANGE THE SCRIPT

Changing how you say things is not very easy. It is helpful to look at it step by step.

Step One
Feel the impact and effect that put-downs have on children and others.

Think about the last time someone put you down. *How did it make you feel?* It might have made you feel inadequate, small, angry, like hiding away, wanting to cry, or perhaps you felt defiant, wanting to assert that you did not care. Why should a put-down make your child feel any different?

What did it make you want to do? Did it make you want to hurt somebody or something, say something hurtful back, or want to shut yourself away? Why should it make your child want to do anything different?

What did you actually do? You might have taken it out on someone else, sent your accuser to 'Coventry', defended yourself verbally, insulted them back, hit them – or done nothing but seethed. Should your children do anything different?

Step Two
Recognise five different types of put-down.

Criticisms are a form of judgement. A child who is subjected to constant criticism gets the message not only that you are disappointed by her but also that you do not like who she is and what she does. You want her to be different. You want her to do whatever it is in the way you would have done it. In other words, you want her to be like you. If you try to turn someone else into yourself, it can mean that you desperately need to love yourself, but do not. Criticism is a means of control. You cannot give someone the space or time to do things their own way. You have to intervene at regular intervals to maintain your control, to mark out your territory.

Straitjackets are statements about a person which lock them into a personality or a role (*'You always . . .'*, *'You are just like . . .'*, *'You will never . . .'*), not allowing them a chance to be different and not giving them the benefit of the doubt. All people, but especially children, develop and change. It is extremely unfair to get fixed ideas about someone and force that role or image on them often in the face of the evidence. Straitjackets can encourage children to become whatever it is you say they are. They live up to, or down to, their image. The straitjacket can become a self-fulfilling prophecy.

Straitjackets come in two forms. *Labels* describe what the child is (*'You are useless, a moron, an idiot, lazy, untidy'*) and what they are not (*'You will never be any good at school, sport, drawing . . .'*, *'Why don't you ever . . . tell the truth, do what I tell you, finish anything . . . ?'*). *Comparisons* involve the child being measured against someone else, a brother or sister (*'Ahmed's much . . . cleverer, tidier, more reliable . . . than you'*), a friend (*'Why can't you be honest, like Scott is with his mum?'*) or a parent (*'With that temper, you're going to grow up just like your dad'*). Even where the comparison with a parent is favourable, the child may feel unable to be how she wants to be. First and foremost, she wants to be herself and to have her parents believe the best, not the worst.

Arbitrary behaviour in adults shows to those on the receiving end that their needs are not worth respecting. Unpredictability is a tool to keep others on tenterhooks, to keep them guessing and waiting, making them focus their energies on the volatile character, trying to read the signs for when the next flare-up will be and trying to placate and keep things calm.

Blame, sarcasm and ridicule are all forms of criticism, so the comments above also apply to this type of put-down.

Anger and shouting count as put-downs because they both suggest that the adult is right and the child is wrong. Each of them is a tool of power used by adults. In summary, any tactic which is used as a tool of power and control can be deployed as a put-down.

Step Three
Understand why you might use put-downs.

When we put children down, we usually believe that we are reacting to *their* behaviour. We therefore hold *them* in some way responsible for what we say. If we say nasty things, it is because they have done something nasty. This is a very comfortable way for us to look at our behaviour. It allows us to avoid responsibility for what we do. But probably every time we say something there will be another form of words we could have used which would have got the same message across. We do not have to be nasty. We, not they, are responsible for what we say, and what words we use to express our disapproval.

In fact, how we respond in these situations is influenced more by how we feel about ourselves. We put other people down because, for a small moment, it makes us feel better about ourselves. Afterwards, we might feel enormously guilty but at the time it makes us feel:

- stronger, superior, and reminds us that we hold some power; in other words, we are in a position to tell off, to pass judgement on another
- better, just by comparison, because we have made someone feel worse
- less embarrassed by, and less responsible for, that person's behaviour. Children's behaviour is widely seen as a measure of how 'good' a parent we are. We don't want to seem to accept behaviour which we feel reflects badly on us, particularly when we are in company. We want to say: *'Don't think that I am anything to do with this!'* So we distance ourselves from the child by telling him off and putting him down.

> We care more about what others think of us than what
> our child thinks of himself

Sometimes we use put-downs because those are the words
our parents used to us. There can be a feeling of comfort in
returning to the familiar, however bad we felt when these
things were said to us.

Being 'in charge' of our children is often interpreted as
being in control. If we feel we are losing that control, we
might find it easier to belittle and humiliate our children
than to confront the more difficult issue of rediscovering
our confidence and reasserting our responsibility and
authority, especially if we were put down a lot as a child.

Once we understand why we fall into the habit of using
put-downs, we should find it easier to avoid them.

Step Four
Realise afterwards when you have said the wrong thing.
Nothing can be changed unless you recognise it first.

Step Five
Hear yourself saying it while you are saying it, when you are
in full flood.

'*I hear myself saying it but I can't stop myself.*' At least the
error is recognised. You can always apologise for what you
have said and withdraw it, for example: '*I think I went a bit
too far then. I didn't mean that.*' Then you should decide what
you *could* have said instead to say what you meant less
harmfully – *and speak it*. Practise it, whispered if necessary,
but you must get used to what it feels and sounds like to say
the new script.

Step Six

Stop yourself before you begin and substitute a more acceptable form of words.

Now that you have practised the alternative words, you know what you can say and it will be easier to slip them in. They may sound strange at first, but it should not be long before you reach the final stage and – most of the time – they come naturally.

Step Seven

Finally the reprogramming will be complete and the alternative script will be learned and will come naturally.

Congratulations! You have made it. And you probably feel much better about yourself for having made the change, and therefore in less need to put others down!

Each step taken will be something to be proud of. It will not necessarily be a smooth process. Like children's changes, there can be two steps forward and one step back, particularly when you are feeling stressed or not feeling very confident. Being realistic, you are unlikely to remove completely the hurtful phrases from your repertoire. But if you can cut them down, recognise when you have been horrid and make amends for it, and take every suitable opportunity in between to raise your child's self-esteem, you should have made enough impact to initiate an upward spiral of improving behaviour on both sides.

Some common put-downs follow, with some alternative, neutral ways of expressing the same feelings alongside. Where relevant, the put-down is also presented in its more demeaning question form, to show it forces a child to agree and puts him on to the defensive.

PUT-DOWNS WHICH UNDERMINE SELF-ESTEEM

Put-downs	**Alternatives**
Attaching labels	
You're useless. Why are you so useless?	It wasn't so smart to clean your boots without covering the floor.
You are so clumsy.	You've got so much going on in your head, you're too busy to look where you're going!
Rejection	
I can't take you anywhere.	I don't like how you behave when we go out. I know you can do better than that.
Why do you always embarrass me?	People don't like children when they behave like that. Don't you like me talking to my friends?
I wish you had never been born.	It can be hard understanding why you do it.
Why don't you go and live with your dad?	We need some cooling-off time. Let's go into separate rooms and we'll talk again in thirty minutes.
Threats	
I'll throw you out if . . .	When you behave like that, it makes you hard to live with. What is it you feel isn't going right?

Put-downs	Alternatives
I'll send you away . . .	That behaviour is not acceptable. Do you realise how angry it makes me?
I'll tell your teacher . . .	I don't think you're proud of what's happened. Let's make sure it doesn't happen again.
Instilling a sense of badness I'll call the police.	You know what you did was wrong.
You're a rotten apple – that's the truth.	Sometimes, I just can't cope: you seem to like getting into trouble.
You'll end up in prison, I'll bet. Why can't you keep out of trouble?	Let's spend more time together. We used to have such fun. What are you doing Saturday?
Lack of respect I don't care what you think/want.	I feel very strongly about this and I'm not prepared to negotiate over it.
Why are you always bothering me?	Now's not a good time. I'll listen better after tea.
Deflating What's so good about that?	You seem pleased with how you have done.
So-and-so did better than that.	Did you do you best? Are you pleased with it?

Put-downs	Alternatives
Lack of trust Where did you get that from? I can never believe you.	That's smart. Is it new or has someone lent it to you?

PUT-DOWNS WHICH UNDERMINE COMPETENCE

Put-downs	Alternatives
I suppose I'll have to do it for you. Why do I always have to do it for you?	You've done well so far. Would you like help with the last bit?
Don't carry that glass jug. You'll drop it.	Keep one hand underneath, then it won't slip and break.
You always give up before you've really tried. Why do you always give up?	Next time you'll get a bit further. It's always hard to start with. Frustrating, isn't it?
You'll never learn. Won't you ever learn?	These things are always harder than you think. Practice makes perfect!
I had to help out when I was your age. Why are you so unhelpful?	I've got a lot on at the moment. I'd love some help – and company.
I was able to cook at your age! Why aren't you practical?	Choose some music and help me do supper. You'll pick up some useful tips.
You always lose/forget things. Why do you always lose things?	Let's think of some ways to help you keep tabs on your coat/PE kit.

7

Discipline, Self-Discipline and Self-Esteem

Discipline is the aspect of child-rearing which causes most parents most heartache. It is also the thing that most parents feel they do not get right. Society and its values have both changed to such an extent that many parents either feel out of touch with traditional approaches or feel little sympathy with them, and are very confused about what they should be doing instead. There is tremendous uncertainty about whether, how and how much we should discipline, and how we can react to limit bad behaviour without playing power and causing an irreparable rift between parent and child.

Under the combined influence of the American, child-centred attitudes of the sixties, and fuelled by the social freedoms preached in the same era, 'discipline' has become something of a dirty word. It is still largely seen as something negative and unpleasant which acts against the interests of children. Viewed as an oppressive instrument of adult power play and control, interfering with the full self-expression and development of the child's individuality, it became – and to a large extent still is seen as – not just 'unfashionable' but also 'old-fashioned'. Yet the replacement, the so-called 'permissive' approach, has not really proved itself to be a practical successor. Parents are beginning to doubt its long-term effectiveness in terms of preparing their children to participate, constructively and contentedly, in society outside the home, and rising juvenile crime and public disorder seem to provide proof.

Overindulgent parenting may not be the only or the correct explanation for rising crime, but parents and policymakers clearly feel they are failing. It is time to look afresh at what we mean by discipline and to construct an approach that achieves four overall aims.

- It must pave the way for children to acquire self-discipline.
- Children must have the space within it to develop self-esteem, self-confidence and self-reliance.
- It must encourage flexibility and initiative to prepare children for living in today's fast-changing world.
- Parents must feel comfortable with it and find it easy to apply.

WHAT IS – OR SHOULD – DISCIPLINE BE ABOUT?

For many people, the word 'discipline' conjures up images of the strict Victorian father wielding a cane. Discipline is inseparable from punishment, and punishment is closely associated with, if not inseparable from, corporal punishment when rules are broken or ignored. Discipline is therefore about power and obedience, and about rule by fear. This is what some people think discipline *should* be like, and it is also the reason so many others went in the opposite direction to reject it. If this is the model we are to reimpose on our children, turning the clock back, we will not give our children the tools to make a success of their lives.

If rule by fear is not an acceptable model of discipline, what is? Is there something in between the traditional, authoritarian style and total permissiveness? What is discipline really about? Why do children need it and parents need to apply it? If it is so important, will any kind of discipline do? What approach does give young people the right skills to thrive and survive in today's world?

Discipline in its best sense can and should be seen as a positive and constructive force. It is the help adults give to children so they can learn how to control and manage their behaviour. It involves making clear how we expect our children to behave in different situations – setting out behaviour guidelines, or limits and boundaries – restricting and prohibiting certain things, not for the sake of it but to achieve some very important objectives. Discipline is also necessary to:

- keep children safe
- teach children to think of others, including their parents
- provide a predictable and therefore secure environment for children to operate in
- help children develop a constructive independence
- make clear the difference between acceptable and unacceptable behaviour
- demonstrate that actions have consequences
- aid the smooth running of any group, for example, the family or school

Discipline, therefore, confers practical advantages. It should not be seen as a negative, punitive concept but as a positive and *enabling* tool for creating consistency, predictability, security and the right environment for (as its source, 'disciple', suggests) teaching and learning. It should not rely on, or be about, wielding power: commanding obedience, handing out punishment and maintaining absolute control like a dictator. As explained in Chapter Three, playing power with children teaches them the same game and invites them to copy our, or to devise their own, power responses. All children need boundaries, to help them control and manage their behaviour. But our target should be discipline without dictatorship – discipline based not on power and deference, but on fairness, legitimate authority and mutual respect.

What are boundaries?

It helps to start by thinking in terms of the negative – of being 'out of bounds'; beyond, or outside, the boundary is forbidden territory where you are not allowed to tread. Being inside the boundary is safe and allowed. But when psychologists use the concept, they do not use it in a geographical or territorial sense. They are talking about the point at which certain behaviours are allowed and not allowed. It is therefore the meeting point between right and wrong, not in some high moral sense, but what individual parents have decided they want, or do not want, their children to do in particular instances. Boundaries are therefore rules and expectations governing behaviour that create a kind of perimeter fence, or limit, beyond which we do not expect our children to go – but within which they are free to act as they please.

Boundaries as a 'play pen'

Children are safe in a play pen; and they can choose what to play within it. At the beginning they do not know how to, or cannot, climb out. But as they grow, they will realise that they have the skill to escape, and they are rightly proud of this. We trust them not to climb out. When they do, we put them back enough times for them to get the message, until we need to redraw the boundaries and offer a larger play space.

Parental authority and responsibility

Creating boundaries for behaviour within which there is scope for choice, growth and development involves exercising *authority* and *responsibility*. We cannot expect children to do what we say without taking responsibility for deciding in advance, and stating clearly, what behaviour we expect or will accept. We cannot expect them to take the rules seriously if we do not take responsibility for monitoring their behaviour so we can comment favourably when they keep within the rules and take action if they regularly ignore them. Nor can we expect them to respect and trust us if we have not demonstrated our authority by setting an example and by expecting, rather than enforcing, compliance.

You and your partner: the importance of presenting a united front

It helps enormously if you and your partner can agree on what the rules are. A united front is far more convincing, and therefore effective, than a divided one. If you and your partner cannot agree on them all, you can:

- select, say, the four areas which are most important to you both and compromise, if necessary, to agree on this core group
- share out the lower-priority issues between you: *'We do this your way, and that my way'*
- agree that whoever is 'in charge' at any one time handles any difficulties without interference from the other unless invited

Any differences of attitude or approach should be discussed in private, and not in front of the child unless you feel his interest is immediately at stake. Differences are often exploited, and create divided loyalties for the children that they will find extremely difficult to manage.

You should not expect to get or to have agreement on everything. It is natural that we will have different expectations, based on the different ways we were brought up. Also, sometimes, we get wound up about an issue and go too far. It is important, then, to hear what someone else says about other ways of handling things. This also means that if you disagree with what your partner is doing, *and you think your child's immediate or long-term interests are at stake*, it is vital that you have the confidence to say so and to forget the rule about the united front.

Important things to remember are:

- all children need some boundaries and routines
- all children should have the experience of certain behaviour being expected of them
- it is better to have just a few rules, and to stick to them, than too many which are constantly ignored
- the age of your child – don't set them up to fail by asking too much of them.

WHICH STYLE OF DISCIPLINE BEST MEETS OUR OBJECTIVES?

Everyone has his or her own style of discipline, or parenting. ('Parenting style' includes and reflects discipline style.) Three core styles can be identified.

The *autocratic* style is usually associated with a traditional, adult-centred regime in which there are many rigid boundaries drawn, without much discussion, around negatives – 'thou shalt not . . .'. The home tends to be tightly organised and parental power reigns supreme.

At its best, the autocratic household can offer a highly secure regime; but at its worst it can be very arbitrary. New rules can be imposed without warning or without appropriate justification or reference to criteria of fairness, if it suits the adults. It can all too easily develop into a 'Jump when I say so!' power game, the parents checking regularly that they still have a hold on the child and others around them by requiring immediate compliance.

In a home in which there are lots of fixed rules, there is little opportunity for a child to make choices, experiment, make mistakes and therefore to find out about himself. Adults determine what the child is allowed to do. If obedience is valued, the child is accepted only if he is 'good', abiding by someone else's view of what is desirable, and is not accepted for himself. Making mistakes – essential for developing creativity, flexibility and self-reliance – is seen either as not conforming or as failing to come up to standard, and is likely to be punished as unacceptable.

In authoritarian homes, adults get their way regardless of the wishes and interests of the child. Little or no respect is shown for the impact of the rule or decision on the child, or for the child's need for a degree of self-determination. Differences of opinion result in clashes not compromise, and clashes produce resentment and ultimately withdrawal. Children in authoritarian families learn to play the same power game as the parents.

The child raised in such a home may be able to fit in to society. But doing as he is told and only as he is told, fearing authority and punishment and being unable to exercise initiative will teach him what he can get away with, will hinder the growth of self-discipline and damage the ability to be creative and flexible. This child will be filled with self-doubt and may become authoritarian himself in order to mask this.

The *permissive* style is at the other end of the spectrum. In permissive, child-centred homes, there are no clear boundaries. The child is indulged and calls the shots. The parent has neither power nor authority.

Here, the boundaries constantly change. There is no consistency. The child *will* test the limits and will *always* go for more, trying to find out where the boundaries are. The boundaries shift, and are usually found on each occasion when the adult has finally had enough and goes berserk. The environment can, then, be highly unpredictable and highly charged, and the child will never really know where she stands. The insecurity and confusion will be intensified by the parent switching between the permissive and the autocratic models when they see that 'things have got out of hand' and they need to reassert control, and then switching back again when they cannot keep it up and see that that does not work either.

The child in this home will have far too many choices.

She gets what she wants. Far from giving her a healthy sense of autonomy, of being in control of herself and being trusted, she will actually feel she is also in control of the adults. This excessive power will not only make her feel uncomfortable and insecure, it will also teach her little about herself. Getting her own way on most things will not teach her to prioritise or to develop judgement. Seeking out the boundary point where someone finally says 'no' means that she demands things that do not accurately reflect her real wishes or interests. She does not have to decide what is really important to her. Also, not being used to hearing or responding to 'no', she does not experience disappointment.

This child is not encouraged to develop any sensitivity to other people's needs. She thinks only of herself and learns to manipulate (this is sometimes dressed up more respectably as negotiation) in order to get her way, ignoring objections to her demands.

Fitting in will be hard and the root insecurity generated by floppy boundaries and inconsistency means that change can be petrifying. Fear of change can numb and paralyse.

The *democratic* approach lies somewhere in between. This offers fewer, firm but flexible boundaries within which there is mutual respect and freedom to explore and to make mistakes. The rules are not just negative but define both rights and responsibilities; and the parent relies much more on natural authority than on the tools of power.

The basic framework is predictable, but there is freedom within the rules, which are not adult-centred. Instead, they define both the rights and the responsibilities of everyone in the social unit. Alterations can be made to the boundaries where appropriate, but only after discussion, and the changes will not, therefore, appear as arbitrary.

There is plenty of scope for choice here, but within clear limits. The choices made available to the child are 'managed' and appropriate in terms of both the child's age and what the parent is prepared to make happen. Choices also make any restrictions elsewhere easier to bear. Through choices and the exercise of priorities, children learn to develop their own rules.

Rights and feelings are acknowledged by both sides. The child therefore not only feels respected but also learns to respect and anticipate the interests of others. Through the process of agreeing who gets what and when, and trading interests, the child learns to *reason* and to *compromise*. Where authoritative decisions are taken, the child can more easily accept that they are taken in his own best interests and knows that in other situations, where it is appropriate, he has an opportunity to state his interests.

This child has to fit in with authority but his own rights have been respected. His environment has been consistent and rule-related but not stiflingly so, with the freedom to express himself and to develop his skills and confidence. Mistakes can be made and, being more secure and confident himself, he is able to manage change and take risks.

'Democratic discipline' clearly scores best. It is better able to supply the conditions conducive to the development of self-esteem, self-confidence, self-reliance and flexibility. The chart on page 174 provides a summary of this analysis.

Does 'democratic discipline' also deliver the first of the four objectives – good self-discipline?

Discipline styles and the development of self-esteem

	Consistent *versus* arbitrary environment	Choice and independence	Compromise and consultation	Parental power play and control	Nagging and criticism
Scope for ☞					
Leads to ☞	Security	Self-esteem, confidence	Mutual respect	Inequality	Self-doubt
Styles of Discipline					
'AUTOCRATIC' Traditional style, rigid Adult-centred 'Thou shalt not.' Tightly organised home *Many tight boundaries*	At best, a consistent and secure environment where everyone knows their place. At worst . . . very arbitrary. Beware the drill sergeant: 'Jump when I say so!'	Very little choice 'Do what I say you can do'. Child has less chance to find out who she is Child accepted only if she sticks to the rules	Very little consultation Clash rather than compromise, leading to resentment Little chance to show trust or respect Child learns to play the same tricks of power and control	Very high control, and the potential for abuse DANGER! Lots of rules can mean lots of failures at living by them	. . . for both parents and children
'DEMOCRATIC' Freedom within rules Rules define the rights and responsibilities of everyone *Fewer, flexible but firm boundaries*	Basic structure of framework predictable Alterations possible, discussed and *not* arbitrary	Plenty, but within limits Appropriate and managed choice Child accepted for who she is	Plenty, but within limits Rights and feelings are acknowledged Child learns to accept others' boundaries Child learns to reason and compromise	You are their equal but you are the adult Parent is a figure of authority ie holds *legitimate* power Less chance of abuse if child allowed to challenge on merits	Should be less criticism Fewer rules, clearly stated Child given space *to be themselves, and to make mistakes,* within the boundaries
'PERMISSIVE' Child-centred, indulgent Give in a lot *No clear boundaries*	No consistency Highly unpredictable 'The boundary is when I flip my lid!' Child tests the limits always goes for more Child never knows where she stands	Too much choice Child never has to prioritise and judge Child given too much power = insecurity	Very little Child used to getting her own way Not sensitive to *your* rights and needs Child learns to manipulate and negotiate	Parent has neither power nor authority Child is in control and holds the cards	No clear expectations, therefore lots of nagging and criticism You step in when it goes too far . . . and it always does!

DISCIPLINE STYLES AND THE DEVELOPMENT OF SELF-DISCIPLINE

One of the main purposes of raising children in a framework of discipline is to encourage self-discipline. Parents cannot have influence for ever. At the end of the day, children have to become responsible for themselves. What is the connection between discipline and self-discipline? Is it possible to develop self-imposed discipline later without early discipline imposed by adults? Will any kind of discipline experience produce self-discipline? If not, what, in particular, is it about early experiences of discipline which help us to develop self-discipline? What is the connection between discipline and morality? This is a book for parents, not moral philosophers, but we need to have some idea of the answers in order to act in a manner which achieves the outcome we want.

There seem to be three components to self-discipline. These are: *habit*, or 'routinised' behaviour (doing things such as hanging your coat up when you come in or always doing homework before TV, without taking a specific decision); *self-interest and self-restraint*, being able to do without immediate pleasures in order to achieve greater personal rewards later (such as studying for exams); and the ability to make *moral judgements* – to appreciate the value of doing things for the benefit of other people, individually or collectively, even if it is not in your own interest – and to develop a personal code of behaviour.

Self-discipline therefore requires that we:
- think ahead, and appreciate the wider consequences of different actions
- accept responsibility for our actions

- have a clear idea about what is good for ourselves and others
- are able to make our own rules
- are able to stick to the rules, made by ourselves or others, and be sufficiently focused to see things through
- trust our own judgements
- are able to accept disappointment

For all these things to happen, we need to have a clear identity and positive sense of ourselves. As has been argued, only some forms of discipline foster good self-esteem. 'Discipline', of itself, is not enough. Having good personal and work habits or routines helps, but does not go far enough. 'Knowing', in the sense of being told, the difference between right and wrong is not enough either: 'knowing' does not mean we will *choose* to do right, and true self-discipline means that we should be able to evaluate such things for ourselves. But to have self-discipline we do need experience of 'task commitment' or 'stickability', of seeing something through to the end. We also need to have had other people's approval and support for our judgements so that we begin to trust ourselves and do things because we want to do them, not because someone else has told us to and will be pleased if we comply.

Which form of discipline is best at producing self-discipline?

Children should have some experience of routines, but it is not in their longer-term interests to be dominated and over-regulated by these. They need to have the consequences of their behaviour made clear to them, and to take responsibility for what they decide to do. They need adult help in meeting long-term commitments, so they experience the pleasure of working towards and achieving a goal that minimises the experience of failure – *stickability*. Finally, children must be offered an environment of mutual trust and respect in which to develop their own appropriate judgements and be trusted and approved of for these. The traditional model of strict discipline cannot provide all these experiences; neither can the 'soft' options.

The winner, once again, is democratic discipline – offering the desirable mix of rules, routines, guidance, support, commitment, freedom and choice.

Putting democratic discipline into effect

Having looked at three of our overall objectives, we must now consider the last. Is it easy to apply?

The discipline contract
There are two parties to the good behaviour agreement – you, and your child. It can be presented as a contract. We should not expect children to behave well if we do not meet them at least halfway. To make discipline work for you, you might consider the following code of behaviour as a way to fulfil *your* side of the contract:

Be fair
Being fair is the best way to avoid resentment and to gain your child's respect. Don't make her suffer for your bad mood, and keep things in proportion.

Be clear

State the rules and the likely consequences of breaking them clearly and in advance. Think ahead. If you are failing to plan, you are planning to fail! If you have not made the rule clear beforehand, let the issue go and apply it next time.

Be firm

Whatever rules you make, stick to them, eight or nine times out of ten, but room for flexibility is important.

Be positive

Praise and rewards work better than punishment. Let your child know you've noticed when she has tried hard, and give her plenty of cuddles.

Be creative

Try to divert her if you see trouble brewing – 'a confrontation avoided is better than a battle won'; compromise; or move your special vase to safety.

Be sensitive

Remember her age, and don't ask for more than she can deliver; apologise if you get it wrong.

Give time

Don't let bad behaviour be the only way of getting your attention.

Offer choices

This will make any restrictions in other areas easier to accept.

PUNISHMENT AND DISCIPLINE: THE LINK

Discipline, as we have seen, is not the same thing as punishment. Setting out guidelines is a very different process from meting out punishments. Children almost always respond better to positive comments about their behaviour than to punishment. However, punishment can be necessary on occasions because:

- it teaches cause and effect. It helps children to realise that their actions have consequences – for other people and for themselves
- it makes children take responsibility for their behaviour. If they take the decision to do something, knowing it to be wrong, they must shoulder that responsibility and be prepared to accept the penalty
- it reinforces the lines which we draw between right, or acceptable, and wrong, or unacceptable, behaviour. It shows that we mean business

There are some widely accepted *principles* that help to keep punishment effective: it must fit the crime (and don't forget that neither thoughtlessness nor accidents are crimes); it must relate to the wrongful act and not to the person; it should be consistent (in other words, the same offence should have the same consequence each time and not be ignored sometimes though not others); and it must not humiliate.

Punishment without humiliation – why is this important?

The punishment that we use should never humiliate a child. If we punish children in a way that also humiliates them, we are using an unnecessary degree of power. Humiliation undermines the person, damages self-esteem and leads inevitably to resentment, antagonism, hostility and, if it continues unabated, to an eventual withdrawal from the relationship.

Punishments that humiliate do not work long-term. They are self-defeating. A child who feels unfairly treated will find other ways to get his own back, even if he does what you force him to do at the time. It will encourage a shoulder-shrugging indifference instead of constructive reflection, teach a child the importance of not getting caught, and convey nothing about how to accept responsibility and develop self-control and self-restraint.

A far more constructive approach to punishments is to see them as 'consequences'. When the 'consequence' is linked and relevant to their action, children are able to view it clearly as a response to their behaviour, not aimed at them personally. Humiliating punishments, on the other hand, such as putting soap in a child's mouth or being made to stand outside in the rain, seem intended solely to shame them. Any child will be more able to change their behaviour than who they are, so it makes practical sense to avoid humiliation and keep any practical or emotional outcome (any feelings of guilt or shame) clearly focused on the act itself.

Isn't all punishment humiliating?

Of course, non-physical punishments can be unpleasant if intended to humiliate and induce guilt, and hurtful shouting can constitute emotional abuse. One child was degraded by having to sit at the family mealtime naked. But punishment need not belittle, hurt, physically or emotionally degrade, or otherwise undermine the person in any way. The purpose of punishment is to teach something and its effectiveness does not depend on humiliation; indeed, it is more likely to be effective if it does *not* humiliate. Children often feel humiliated and insulted when they are punished harshly, especially when they are hurt physically, and there are many alternatives to smacking which are far less severe and far more appropriate to the kind of negative behaviour that young children display. If useful lessons are learnt from a well-chosen 'consequence' it is unlikely to have been a very upsetting experience. It is always valuable to think clearly and honestly about what lessons a child will learn from any punishment – and also to consider why they behaved in a way that annoyed you in the first place.

To smack or not to smack?

Smacking may stop a child immediately, but it is almost never the best way to stop a child from doing something again, a far more important target. If you deal only with the immediate incident, it means that you are repeatedly reacting and punishing, each time it occurs. It gets you nowhere. Punishing children in this way is unhelpful. It teaches them how to avoid getting caught. It also completely fails to teach them how to change their behaviour, to understand why it might be in their interests to change it, or to give them any good reason for wanting to change it. When overused, punishments have to get tougher to stay effective. Smacking can be a slippery slope to more physically damaging responses.

An American researcher has recently reviewed the results of eighty-four separate studies of corporal punishment across many countries. She found clear and consistent evidence that corporal punishment is linked to undesirable outcomes. For example, she found that it increases the incidence of aggressive behaviour both in children and later when they become adults; it impairs children's mental health and increases their chance of being victimised by bullies; and it interferes with the development of children's ability to think and assess their behaviour in a moral framework.

'But Mum, you're supposed to look after me!'

These immortal words were said by a distraught and disbelieving two-year-old on being smacked for the first time. She clearly felt utterly betrayed. The first assumption of her life – that the person on whom she depended totally for survival would always protect her from harm and deliver care – had been shattered. Her trust had been thrown into question. She ran to her mother, who had delivered the smack, for consolation for her grief.

Her feelings, if not her words, will be repeated within every child in every similar situation. To hurt your own child is something we are all tempted to do on occasion. But it is something a child will never understand because, in their eyes, you are supposed to love and care. If you, the parent, are not 'on their side', who else will be? It marks the beginning of a rift which will get increasingly difficult to heal. If a child thinks you do not care for her, why should she care about what you think?

Smacking usually makes things worse

Smacking is also best avoided because it does not work. Many children use bad behaviour either to get attention or to gain control. Punishment *is* that desired attention and, by making us stop what we are doing to give the punishment, is the process of regaining control. Sometimes, then, punishment will actively encourage children to reoffend.

Smacking is an act of power. It might frighten a child into submission but the child is likely to get his own back some other way. For every put-down there is a pay-back. Smacking fuels the power battle; it rarely ends it.

Smacking does not usually 'fit the crime'

Smacking is usually, though not always, done on impulse. It is hard to control the force of the blow when we are at breaking point. Often it is 'the last straw', a relatively minor thing, which causes us to lash out and reflects our mood rather than the seriousness of the behaviour. Smacking, then, almost never fits the crime. It happens when we 'go over the top'. When any kind of punishment is out of proportion to the offence, a child will feel ferociously angry and resentful. Her first desire will be either to get even or to withdraw.

If we smack when we are in full control, we still have to think whether to hit and hurt even mildly is the right response to negative behaviour. The only circumstance in which it seems justified to smack a child is to stop them immediately from doing something that is likely to hurt or endanger them significantly more, such as running out into the road, and when there is not the time to explain or to deal with it gently.

Smacking is arbitrary

Impulse means that we do not plan it. If we cannot predict our own behaviour, our children certainly cannot. Our lashing-out is unexpected, arbitrary and, to a child, usually completely incomprehensible, causing more anger, outbursts and resentment.

Smacking does not teach 'morality'; it stops children from acquiring moral sensitivity

Far from teaching morality by clarifying what is right and wrong, frequent smacking and other forms of harsh and humiliating punishment can permanently damage children's developing capacity for moral thinking by stunting their growing sense of responsibility and empathy. If children are most often smacked without warning when adults are angry, they are unlikely to be clear about what it was they did wrong, especially if they weren't punished in that way for the same 'offence' on the previous occasion. When there is no obvious link between the action and the outcome (the punitive smack), it will be hard either to anticipate what might happen and therefore accept that the action is wrong and take responsibility for it, or to accept that the 'consequence' is justified. If you also habitually blame your child unfairly – for breaking the dish you should have removed, spilling the drink you overfilled, or even for your headache – you confuse the issue of personal responsibility even further. A child who ends up feeling responsible for everything will be unable to perceive a genuine responsibility for anything; and when you then ignore or deny your child's upset and confusion, you teach him similarly to ignore others' feelings, further undermining his moral awareness.

Punishment options that avoid causing physical hurt

There are plenty of 'consequences', alternatives to physical punishment, that many parents find effective, such as:

- withdrawal of privileges: e.g., going out with friends (being 'grounded'), staying up later at the weekends, sweets
- restricted use of television, computer, bicycle or other valued activity for a short period
- removal of a favourite toy
- withdrawal of pocket money for a limited period
- sending the child to their room
- sending to a 'cooling-off' place which is different from their bedroom: it could be the corner of a room, a particular chair, or halfway down the hall or up the stairs
- sending to bed early
- a verbal telling-off

The punishment contract

Be clear
Give clear advance warning of what the likely punishment will be. If you have not made things clear in advance, it is better to let the incident pass and clarify the rules for next time.

Be fair
Ensure the punishment fits the crime: that it is reasonable, appropriate, and not out of proportion to it. Wherever appropriate, agree the punishments with your child in advance, so they are seen to be reasonable and are accepted.

Be sensitive
Make it clear that it is the behaviour that is unacceptable, not the child: *'That was a stupid thing to do!'* not *'You are so stupid!'*

Be brief

Apply the punishment as soon as possible after the offence and complete it quickly. *'Spend half an hour in your room'* is better than *'You will miss your favourite TV programme for the next three weeks.'* However justified that kind of penalty seems at the time, delays and time to replay and reinvent the incident allow resentment to take root.

Be loving

Forget the incident once the punishment is over (easier said than done, but try) and give her a reassuring cuddle to show that you still love her.

Be focused

Do not pile on complaints about other behaviour at the same time. They are irrelevant to the issue at hand; they will send negative messages to the child about how you feel about her; they will act as fertile ground for resentment.

Be firm

Apply the punishments consistently, so she knows what to expect.

All forms of punishment should be used as little as possible

The more we punish, the more we tell our child that she is 'bad'. The more we give her this message, the more she will think that we do not like her. The more she sees herself as 'bad', the more she is likely to live up to the image and behave in bad ways, eventually relishing the notoriety and remaining uninfluenced by the escalating punishments.

The more we convince her we do not like her, the less she will try to please and behave as we wish. The more she gives up trying to please, the less chance we have of successfully changing her behaviour. The more we damage her self-esteem, the more likely she is to 'put down' others, which may eventually get her into trouble with the law.

Think first! Before you punish, think about whether the behaviour that has annoyed you was an accident, the result of thoughtlessness or mischievousness, or intentional bad behaviour. *Most people behave best in a happy, tolerant and understanding atmosphere in which they feel liked and approved.*

Why do we find it difficult to say 'no'?

Saying 'no' to children is not always easy or pleasant. Sometimes, it is very hard work, and we cannot face the struggle. Most of us at some time will find ourselves saying 'yes' when we know we should have said 'no'. Some people almost never say 'no'. But the funny thing is that the more you are prepared to say 'no', and mean it and enforce it, the less you have to use it. Children get the message. Parents who have to say 'no' for most of the day will probably admit that they are not enforcing it. They give in too soon, so children get a mixed message about what they are and are not allowed to do. There are many reasons why we find it difficult to say 'no'. However, there are some common patterns which we all display at some time or other. Have a look at the list overleaf. Do you recognise any one, or more than one, of the reasons applying specially to you?

- We want to protect our child from the 'pain', or discomfort, of disappointment.
- We want to protect ourselves from facing his feelings of anger or disappointment.
- We want to avoid the responsibility of taking a decision about an issue.
- We want to avoid apparently being in a position of power or control.
- We want to keep the peace and fear the row, or other consequences, which may follow.
- We need our child's approval, want to be his friend, and fear his rejection.
- We want to keep the times we are with our child free from conflict.

We can get the necessary strength, confidence and authority to say 'no' when it matters by understanding these reasons more fully.

Protecting your child from the pain of disappointment

Of course, it hurts to see those we love suffer, but mild or modest discomfort and disappointment are facts of life. Children will be better equipped to cope with the realities of life if they experience and learn to manage disappointment, which we often see as pain, especially that of not always getting their own way. This does not mean that we should go out of our way to expose them to pain. It does mean that being the cause of their disappointment is not something about which we need to feel guilty or ashamed. Being used to accepting 'no', and realising that they can survive the disappointment, makes them stronger in the face of adversity and also gives them a better idea of which 'wants' are really important to them. Going without from time to time helps to develop both a sense of priorities and a sense of identity.

Protecting ourselves from our child's feelings of anger or disappointment

We often avoid saying 'no' to protect ourselves from having to respond to our children's negative feeling. As parents, we are used to 'making them feel better'; but how can we do this without 'giving in' and sending the feelings away or preventing them in the first place? If we consider we have *caused* the anger or disappointment, what do we do when they display it?

- Stay there.
- Be there.
- Say nothing.
- Talk with touch.

Avoiding the responsibility of taking a decision about an issue

Sometimes we avoid saying 'no' because it involves us in taking a decision about the rights and wrongs of an issue and taking responsibility for that decision afterwards. It is easier to say 'yes', particularly if we don't find it easy to make decisions. Saying 'no' puts the burden on us to have a reason for the refusal, and that involves both thinking the issue through and remaining committed to that decision. If we cannot think of two good reasons for taking that line, then we should at least question the fairness and reasonableness of the decision. We should not always expect to have to supply the reasons to our children. However, as a safeguard, and for their benefit, we would do well to check our reasoning and sense of fairness from time to time.

Avoiding apparently being in a position of power and control

Some people love to play power. Other people hate it. For perhaps political or ideological reasons, they hate to be in a position to control and limit the behaviour of others, even their own children. They believe that saying 'yes' allows children to control their own lives, while saying 'no' amounts to inappropriate and illegitimate interference.

Fearful of the row, or other consequences, which may follow

If you find yourself often avoiding saying 'no' because you are frightened of the power battle or retaliations which will follow if you do, it is time to ask yourself two questions.

- Have I got myself into a power-type relationship with my child, and if so, why?
- Am I not in reality being blackmailed by a threatened emotional backlash?

If the answer to either of these questions is 'yes', then you have to ask yourself two further questions.

- Who is in charge?
- Who should be in charge?

Needing approval, and fearing rejection

Some parents find it hard to say 'no' because they are afraid their child will not like them if they do not give them what they ask for. They need to be liked and to feel that the child is their friend, and also to believe that their child sees them as a friend.

The parent who needs the approval, or friendship, of their child to improve their own sense of self-esteem is giving that child a large and very difficult burden which she should not be asked to carry. For that child, the parent will not be that necessary constant factor, offering guidance and security. Instead, the parent will bend with the whim of the child, passing over to the child responsibility for the parent's happiness. In such relationships, the child is likely to be rejected and made to feel guilty if she exposes any of the feelings of anger and even hatred which go hand in hand with childhood love. It is, however, important that children realise that loving and hating are part and parcel of growing up. Both emotions should be accepted.

Wanting to keep the times you are together free from conflict

It is very hard for a parent who does not spend much time with their child to be tough and cause upset, for it is only natural that you want to keep those precious moments free from conflict. Separated fathers are known to spoil their children rotten when it is their weekend 'on'. Working mums who arrive home near bedtime find it hard to resist the pleas and ploys for more time and attention. Children have a way of knowing about the weak spot, and they usually exploit it for all it is worth – which is usually quite a lot.

But giving in, or being soft, is not in their best interest.

In summary

Children flourish within an ordered framework of clear expectations and boundaries that offers scope for mutual trust and respect alongside structure, consistency and commitment. If we return to strict, Victorian-style obedience and a punitive, or rule-governed, model of discipline, not only will we increase feelings within our children of rejection and resentment, but we will also not give them the experiences which are necessary for them to develop confidence and flexibility and apply self-discipline. Our society will not benefit, and neither will our children.

8

Commitment

Much of what children need in order to grow up secure and happy, and to be strong enough in themselves to be able to give to others, can be summed up in the word 'commitment'. It is similar to the phrase used in business, 'bottom line assessment' on which every parent needs to focus. After all the ups and downs and demands of family life, children need nonetheless to feel that someone has both *made a commitment* to them, and continues to *demonstrate* that commitment, consistently, so they feel there is someone they can rely on to act as their safety net and someone to lean on when they need practical and emotional support to reduce any difficult feelings that could overwhelm them.

Making a commitment to something or somebody is usually understood to mean:

- taking on responsibility for that thing or person
- binding oneself to someone
- acknowledging a sense of duty
- seeing it through

When you have a child, you take on a commitment. It is a significant and demanding commitment. You are responsible both for and to that child. You bind yourself to him or her, and it is inevitable that this will be at some, possibly considerable, cost to yourself. A commitment is, according to the dictionary, an 'engagement that restricts freedom of action'. It reduces your freedom. It requires that you put the child's needs before your own – not always, but enough to let him realise that he can rely on you to have his major needs met.

Showing commitment implies:
- loving
- being interested
- cherishing
- being there
- caring
- offering support
- keeping safe

With commitment, a child will feel valued and welcomed and can bask safely in the warmth of intimacy. Without it he can feel neglected, abandoned, bereft and alone. If it is intermittent and unreliable, he could become withdrawn. From the child's point of view, if the adults, who *made* him, appear not to care, it will be very hard for him to develop a sense of self-respect or pride in who he is. A child's self-esteem relies crucially on whether he believes and perceives that his parents are reliably committed to him and provide him with a close relationship that he can trust.

HOW CHILDREN INTERPRET COMMITMENT

Commitment is demonstrated when parents:

- are there to ask their child about his life, at home and at school
- are willing to see things from the child's point of view
- make sure their child is appropriately fed and clothed
- are tolerant of the common difficulties in each stage of growing up
- give their child rights at the same time as responsibilities
- show respect for their child

Commitment is perceived as uncertain, by implication, when parents:

- are not at home much to be with their child because they have elderly relatives to care for, they spend a lot of time on their own interests or they are out at work
- are at home but are too self-absorbed or not sufficiently interested to play with or talk to him, to be told about his life or his day
- separate or divorce. Unable to understand the subtleties of adult relationships until near maturity, the raw message younger children receive when their parents split up is that the departing parent cannot have loved them enough to want to stay with them. Children generally believe parents should try harder to save the relationship, the notable exception being the presence of obvious violence and instability
- disappear from the scene altogether and lose touch with the child

- find a new partner, and transfer some loyalty and commitment to the new relationship. It is inevitable that at the beginning the 'friend' will be seen as an 'interloper' who makes the parent seem less available and whose own commitment to the child is likely to seem far weaker and less reliable. If there is a conflict of loyalties, someone has to win or lose and the child will feel very vulnerable

WHAT IS THE EFFECT OF UNCOMMITTED PARENTING?

If a child has reason to doubt the commitment of either parent, he can feel so vulnerable and so full of self-doubt as to be unable to trust, or to commit himself subsequently to, anything or any other relationship. To be able to commit to something or somebody, you have to be able to give and to lose something of yourself to it, to identify with it and to say yes, I am like you, or I believe in you, or in that. You have to know yourself. But for people who have not experienced commitment from their parents, this is really hard.

They will be so well-defended against the possibility of further rejection that they will be extremely wary of giving. (Or, alternatively, they will rush into ill-considered relationships or early motherhood in search of love and commitment, mindless of the consequences for existing or future children.) They will feel that nobody else will want them if their own parents have not shown, to their satisfaction, that they were wanted. And they will be reluctant for anybody or any organisation to take, or expect, anything from them.

The greatest danger comes when people who have not experienced commitment find it difficult, in their turn, either to make or demonstrate a commitment to the children they bring into the world. The damaging pattern can then be repeated. If we do not have the experience of committed parenting, we will be less likely to be able to have, manage or sustain mutually fulfilling relationships which require tolerance, resilience, a strong sense of self, and deep reserves of love, giving and forgiveness. With so little confidence, the process not just of giving and sacrifice, but also of having a firm idea of where to draw the boundaries and what guidance to offer, becomes much more difficult. The problem is not lack of morality in any religious sense, but lack of emotional maturity and experience of human caring.

DISCIPLINE, CONSISTENCY AND COMMITMENT

Discipline and consistency go hand in hand. There is no point in having rules and regulations if they are not consistently applied. The great advantage of rules and boundaries is that issues do not have to be argued about every time. Consistently applied, they lose their contentiousness and create peace and security. Responsibility for the rules and any departures from them is clearly taken by the adult. Consistent application of rules, and of punishments where the rules have been infringed, requires a parent to be involved in the comings and goings and activities of their child. Monitoring behaviour requires a commitment. It is not easy to do. It is far easier to avoid the confrontation, opt out and get on with your own life than to make sure your child does not get away with something that infringes rules. But if you do opt out, the hidden message for your child might be that you do not care about him. Lack of consistency and clear rules defining both rights and responsibilities, therefore, sends deeper messages.

Security comes from certainty and consistency equals commitment.

SEPARATION, DIVORCE AND COMMITMENT

Separation or divorce is a painful process for everyone involved, especially children regardless of their age. It is rarely undertaken without a considerable amount of thought. When parents do decide to go their separate ways, there is much that they can do to make the experience less confusing for children.

Of greatest importance, children must be assured that their parents' difficulties have nothing to do with them. They must not be allowed to take on any sense of responsibility or blame for the break-up. It is very common for younger children to believe that they caused the breakdown through naughtiness, for example, and for older children to consider they could or should have stepped in and prevented it in some way, even if they no longer consider themselves directly responsible.

Children will need to be reassured that both of their parents still love them and will be continuing as active parents – being there for them – for as long as the children need them. That relationship should not change. We should not forget that in times of stress children need the security of both parents' love even more; in other words, access should never be denied despite, sometimes, intense feelings of resentment.

They should not be kept in the dark, or lied to, about what is happening, because children's imaginations can conjure a range of frightening scenarios that seem plausible to them when the truth is not made clear. Respecting their right to know about things which directly affect them will help them to manage the changes, to keep a sense of control, and to feel loved, understood and respected by their parents – a sign of the promise of continued 'parenting'.

Whatever anger and resentment may be overtly or covertly expressed between the parents, the children should not be asked to take sides and divide their loyalties. They need to maintain an unfettered commitment to each parent and to expect the same in return. When children are asked to choose between one parent and the other, they can feel split in two psychologically, which may explain why some children in the immediate aftermath prefer to keep it comfortable and refuse to see the non-resident parent. However, most children really benefit from staying in regular touch with both parents, and ways should therefore be found to maintain some contact – even if only by phone or e-mail – to enable a full relationship to resume when everyone is less fraught.

Children need repeated opportunities to express or communicate their concerns and feelings about what is happening. You can either engage them in direct conversation if they seem ready for it and are old enough, or encourage them to get things off their chest through art, sport or in role-play using their soft toys.

To preserve a sense of security and normality during the difficult period of adjustment, it will be helpful to maintain as many daily routines as possible, as well as contact with familiar people such as grandparents or cousins from both sides of the family.

New partners

New relationships are exciting, powerful and absorbing, especially to someone emerging from the ashes of a previous one. They can also be demanding, with each side needing 'proof' of love and commitment. Children are always pleased to see either parent happy again, but at the same time they can feel troubled because at least some of the attention they crave is directed elsewhere, which feels threatening. You might consider the situation advantageous for all concerned; however, your child is more likely to see your availability and commitment as reduced by half, shared with the new partner, at the very time he probably feels he needs almost all of you. If that person then moves on, for whatever reason, and a new relationship blossoms, your child may feel he receives from you only half of that part he felt was remaining previously. In other words, when any new relationship is forming, it is essential to maintain certain times – evenings or at the weekend – that are ring-fenced for your child.

There is no point bemoaning the rate of relationship breakdown. Relationships will continue to fail and parents will continue to separate, though the consequential hurt, confusion, questioning and unhappiness should not be underestimated. It is far more constructive to focus social comment on the need for parents to accept that the end of their legal or common-law relationship does not, and should not, mean the end of being an active and reliable parent for their children, who will continue to have a profound need to be cherished, especially when there are new relationships and new children. Throughout the process of moving apart, and for the years of childhood remaining, what really matters is for each parent to demonstrate, unswervingly, a continuing commitment to each child to preserve his or her self-belief and self-esteem.

OTHER AREAS OF PERSONAL COMMITMENT

Research shows that the experience of feeling confident, or not confident, that a parent is there for you and is committed to you can set a pattern of interaction with others that is often repeated in subsequent relationships and situations throughout life, though this is not set in stone. People tend to be more or less trusting of others, and manage situations more or less defensively or openly, according to how much intimacy, trust and interest they feel they encountered when young. There are four areas where early patterns of commitment can be replayed:

- tasks
- ideas
- organisations
- other people apart from children

Commitment to tasks

In many ways, commitment to tasks – what we might call 'stickability' – is more important than commitment to relationships. Those who find it hard to see a job or task through to the end, even when the task is one they set themselves, will have to live with disappointment, frequent failure, low achievement and probably self-hate. It can become a vicious circle in which one failure feeds the next, because they end up not believing in themselves and not even trying.

Task commitment is an important element in self-discipline. Even when the going gets tough, with self-discipline we can keep to our target. Helping our children when they are young to achieve their own aims and those imposed by others, for example the school, teaches them how to see something through. It shows them the pleasure they can get from achieving. They will also enjoy our approval of their effort. They can then become self-motivated. Our interest is a sign of our commitment to them. If we show no encouragement or interest, why should they bother?

Commitment to ideas

Ideas, beliefs and opinions are expressions of ourselves. When we feel low and unhappy we are often less clear about who we are and do not know what to think. We may therefore be very reluctant to commit to a view in case we want to change it later, either because our view of ourselves may change, or because we do not want to accept the long-term implications of that view. Being unsure, we may also be more susceptible to the influence of others around us. If our social group changes, our views might change, too. Someone who is feeling vulnerable may ask themselves: *'Does this idea fit with who I think I am at the moment?'*

Commitment to organisations

Organisations have identities and also make demands on their members. To commit to an organisation, we therefore have to be able to identify with it and accept that we 'belong' and are similar to other people within it; in other words, we have to have a clear view of ourselves and be willing to lose some of that identity to become one of a crowd. We also have to be prepared to give when and if any demands are made. Whether the organisation is educational, job-related or voluntary, someone with good self-esteem is likely to find it easier to conform and commit than someone who is vulnerable and unsure of themselves.

Sometimes, of course, people with an unclear identity will respond very differently. Instead of holding themselves back from organisations, they will do the opposite. They will seek direction and security in a career or institution that offers them a total way of life. They hand themselves over to the organisation and gain comfort from the fact that all major decisions are taken for them.

Commitment to other people

When you demonstrate that you care for and feel some responsibility to other family members or neighbours by going out of your way for them when they're in need or just because you want to stay in close touch, you not only set an example of what you think is right but also show your children that they can expect something similar from you. It will increase their confidence in your availability to look after them. Showing that you care for your partner, tolerate any individual quirks, are interested in their favourite activities and you celebrate anniversaries sends a similar message – that you are happily committed to a relationship that is in general a source of comfort to all the family.

COMMITMENT AND GOVERNMENT

Government also has a part to play by supporting families in their communities and enabling parents to give as much time and attention as they know children need. Parenting does not happen in a social or political vacuum; poverty and the wider social and physical environment can put heavy pressures on parents trying to raise their children with decency.

Conclusion

We need to redefine and rediscover commitment in parenting. This message is not necessarily easy for parents who are either seduced by the potent temptations of personal and material freedom or severely tested by the daily challenge of living in deprived and downtrodden areas. 'Positive parenting' requires a new contract of commitment from everyone with an interest in improving social cohesion and children's quality of life: from government, from the wider community, as well as from parents.

Conclusion:

'POSITIVE PARENTING' AND THE POSITIVE AND NEGATIVE BEHAVIOUR CIRCLES

THE 'GOOD ENOUGH' PARENT

As I have stressed throughout, having self-esteem is crucially important because it impacts on so much of our life – the quality of our relationships, our ability to know our own minds, our willingness to try new things and expand our horizons, and how we deal with life's disappointments. How we feel about ourselves influences how we behave towards others, both adults and children. Understanding the common behaviour patterns associated with both low and high self-esteem, seeing that hurt can be done when it goes wrong, and realising how good you and your child will feel when it goes right will contribute to your finding a new sense of direction in your parenting.

Diagrams 1 and 2 (see pages 208 and 210) illustrate the relationship dynamics set in motion when you feel either good or bad about yourself. The parent is represented in the small circle in the centre. The child is the outer circle. When people are feeling good, there is a tendency to initiate the behaviour patterns and responses shown in the 'positive circle' (Diagram 1) and reproduce the good feelings in those they live with. When people are feeling low and self-critical, there is a tendency to set the bad patterns in motion using techniques of power reinforcement and control, and create those same bad feelings in others, as shown in the 'negative circle' (Diagram 2). These diagrams represent summaries of all the issues raised in this book. And they reinforce the positive message that it is possible to understand, manage and adapt our behaviour, and move between the circles, regardless of our own childhood experiences, in order to give our children a firm foundation for a fulfilled and happy life.

The diagrams show that we do not *have* to get locked into a negative cycle of passing on our inadequate feelings to our children. It is not a simple process of the child observing and actively copying self-doubt. If that were the case, it would, indeed, be difficult to break the pattern. By being a more complex process than that, by involving the use of social techniques of power and control, and by subtly putting people down so the initiator can feel good, if momentarily, by comparison, it gives us the opportunity to become aware of what we do and to step in and stop ourselves – at least some of the time. Of course, we become quite set in our ways. Of course, some of the responses and techniques we adopt involve echoes from our own childhood. But if we believe that these early experiences somehow control us, and are part of our blueprint, we might give up trying to change from the start, believing it to be a hopeless or endless challenge. We do not need the psychiatrist's couch and a fat bank balance to inspect and identify the very common ways all human beings react to the threat of equality by finding apparent safety in the inappropriate use of power.

THE POSITIVE CIRCLE

Parents with a strong sense of self-worth are quick to notice and to praise and reward good or appropriate behaviour. Appropriate behaviour can be actions which show, for example, kindness, initiative, effort or thinking ahead. 'Good' behaviour will be actions which you have specifically sought, for example, folding pyjamas in the morning, coming home at the agreed time, or sitting at the main table while everyone eats. What is important is that the child's efforts are noticed (not because you are checking on him, but because you have time for him and are not self-absorbed) and commented on, so that he gets some positive feedback.

- Praise, combined with frequent physical and verbal demonstrations of love, helps children to feel approved.
- If parents give children time, and show interest in what they do, it increases their motivation or willingness to work at something, because they do it in part to please their parents. Showing that you think something is important will help your child to attach the same value to the enterprise, whether it is schoolwork, friendships or a leisure activity.
- Opportunities to develop skills and talents will help children to achieve self-confidence and self-awareness.
- Knowing yourself will help you not only to clarify the kind of regime you want for your children but also to enforce it consistently. Consistency demonstrates commitment and creates a secure and predictable environment. Having the strength to say 'no' in the process of enforcing the boundaries consistently reinforces that security.

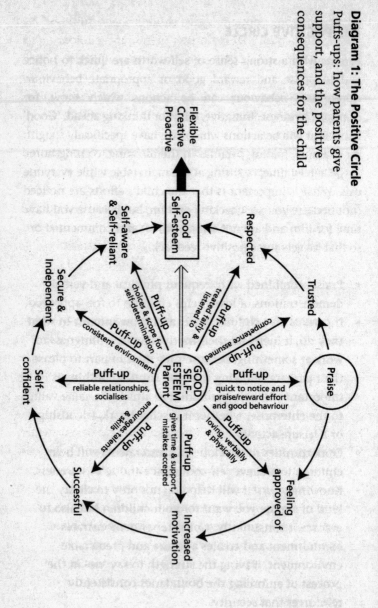

Diagram 1: The Positive Circle
Puffs-ups: how parents give support, and the positive consequences for the child

Flexible
Creative
Proactive

Good Self-esteem

Self-aware & Self-reliant

Respected

Secure & Independent

Trusted

Puff-up
choices & scope for self-determination

Puff-up
treated fairly & listened to

Puff-up
competence assumed

GOOD SELF-ESTEEM Parent

Puff-up
consistent environment

Puff-up
reliable relationships, socialises

Puff-up
quick to notice and praise/reward effort and good behaviour

Praise

Self-confident

Puff-up
encourages talents & skills

Puff-up
gives time & support, mistakes accepted

Puff-up
loving, verbally & physically

Feeling approved of

Successful

Increased motivation

- Being strong enough to give children opportunities for self-determination, letting them make choices about appropriate things, allows them to develop self-reliance.
- Assuming competence, but giving children a safe space within set limits to experiment and make mistakes, shows trust.
- Acknowledging children's rights to be heard and treated fairly demonstrates respect.

Children who feel approved of are aware of their special skills and talents, are trusted and respected, are confident and independent: are children with good self-esteem.

THE NEGATIVE CIRCLE

The dynamics at work in the negative circle operate in the opposite direction. We all know that when we have had a bad day or are very tired, we tend to 'take it out' on someone else. Why do we seem to need to do this, and what form does it usually take?

- When we feel vulnerable, we often get rid of our own feelings of inadequacy by blaming our children for our own or for general mistakes and mishaps in order to protect our fragile self. But this is very unfair. Wherever blame is placed upon children, children will feel guilt and disapproval. Inappropriate blame is a form of destructive criticism which will, eventually, cripple the recipients and render them incapable of testing themselves, of reaching out or going forward.

Diagram 2: The Negative Circle
Put-downs: how parents reinforce their
power and control, and the negative
consequences for the child

Inflexible
Rule-bound
Reactive

Poor
Self-esteem

Self-
criticism

Put-down
rarely praises

Guilt

Put-down
uses emotional
blackmail, 'withdraws'

Blame

Put-down
keeps control through
arbitrary behaviour

Insecure &
dependent

POOR
SELF-
ESTEEM
Parent

Put-down
transfers feelings of
inadequacy to protect self

Self-
doubt

Put-down
assumes incompetence,
ridicules

Put-down
quick to criticise
and punish

Disapproved of

Put-down
plays power and
inclined to debase

Humiliated

Put-down
emphasises failure
and mistakes

Feelings of failure
and inadequacy

- When we feel low, we also tend to emphasise children's failures and mistakes. We are either simply less tolerant of mistakes at these times, or we can begin to feel let down by them, or even responsible for them. This makes us feel uncomfortable and perhaps guilty, so we again pass these feelings over – usually to our nearest and dearest – by focusing on errors and allocating responsibility very clearly away from ourselves. What we are actually saying is, *'I'm no good, and it makes me feel better that you're no good either.'* This further expression and exposure of bad feelings will only add to the swirling, negative cocktail of emotions present and probably lead to even worse reactive behaviour on all sides. But it can have a deeper impact on our children. Anyone who is made to feel generally incompetent will lose the will to try anything: what would be the point? If a child feels she is no good, why should she try again, and suffer the pain of having her nose rubbed in yet another failure?
- Vulnerable parents will also be inclined to punish and behave harshly in a manner that may humiliate their child. Overt demonstrations of physical or emotional power are often covers for feelings of powerlessness inside. A humiliated child is a cowering child who will be storing up not only feelings of anger, resentment and revenge but also layer upon layer of self-doubt.
- Control through the element of surprise is another manifestation of power and a form of put-down. Children who live in an arbitrary environment with constant fear and uncertainty cannot develop the trust and security needed to strengthen and believe in themselves.

THE 'GOOD ENOUGH' PARENT: MOVING BETWEEN THE CIRCLES

The concept of the 'good enough' mother or parent implies that you can be a good parent without being a perfect one; that there should be room to make mistakes, that mistakes are inevitable; and that, provided you are doing enough things right and demonstrate love, the mistakes do not matter or do serious harm. It is an important, useful, and also a comforting idea which can reduce our destructive sense of guilt and help us to cope better.

However, when not fully understood, it can be exploited to justify and excuse behaviour that is neither justifiable nor excusable. It can be used to avoid trying to understand, change or take responsibility for our less attractive behaviour. *'I'll forget what I have just said or done, even though I know it was pretty nasty, because I know I love my child really, so that's OK.'* But this kind of thought is just not good enough! Before we rest on our laurels in the comfort of believing that we have been 'good enough', and have provided a 'safety net' level of care, we need to be crystal clear about how good is 'good enough', and what it is we need to be good at.

What should be measured are love, care and commitment. And what matters is not whether *you think* you are giving these things, but whether *the child perceives* that he is receiving them. Love and care are demonstrated through commitment. You can say you love your child until you are blue in the face, but if you do not also demonstrate it so that he believes you, it will count for very little. Inevitably, then, the exact height of the hooks on which to attach this 'safety net', or hammock, of love and care through which you should not let your child fall will be different in different cases.

If being a 'good enough' parent means demonstrating love and commitment most of the time, it will involve ensuring your child feels competent and happy with himself and is not put down. In practical terms, therefore, it means spending much of your time in the positive circle rather than the negative circle. It also means recognising quite quickly when you have strayed into the negative one, and knowing how to manage your behaviour while you are there so that you can move out again. For example:

- When you are feeling upset about something, at a low ebb, and get bad-tempered, instead of blaming your child and making him feel bad, you can take responsibility for your mood. *'I've had an awful day and I'm in a foul mood. I'd steer clear of me for an hour if I were you!'* After this warning, if you do snap, the child is less likely to take it personally.
- Instead of putting your child down and shrugging it off, because you think you are good enough, you can quite easily repair the damage and make reparation by doing or saying something which restores his self-esteem and faith in himself and your love for him. Implementing 'The Expertise' (see Chapter Five) and showing lots of appreciation and approval, spending time with him, showing pride and interest in his skills, and thereby getting the warm glow of positive feedback from him about how much he values your time and commitment, are all techniques to use to switch across from the negative to the positive circle of behaviour which reinforces trust, respect, love and attention.
- Try to improve your own self-image from time to time. Keeping on the positive track may sometimes require

more than merely saying and doing the right thing for
them.

Most of us move between the circles. We have good days
and bad days. A 'not good enough' parent is one who:

- strays and stays in the negative circle for prolonged
  periods of time
- finds it hard to accept any measure of equality in the
  relationship
- finds it hard to accept any responsibility for
  commitment
- fails to demonstrate authority, only using the language
  and tactics of power, which increase inequalities

In summary

Being a parent is, for most people, their greatest challenge.
Children can give us our best moments, but they can also
bring us face to face with our worst moments. Managing the
emotional storms which are often unleashed, from our side as
well as theirs, takes patience, a great deal of understanding,
and even more skill.

Positive parenting is important. We know that how we
parent can have a powerful effect on a child's future – on
his happiness, on his ability to learn, on his willingness
to live within a structured framework, and on his chances
of having sustained and fulfilled relationships. Having
positive self-esteem is central to achieving these aims; for
children thrive when parents acknowledge and respond to
their needs. We need to improve our understanding of why
we behave as we do. We need to develop skills to manage

the changes, stresses and conflicts that characterise parenthood.

Effective parenting is not intuitive and it is not learned overnight. Positive parenting requires a new contract of commitment from everyone who cares about the quality of life for our children and the future of our society. With continued support from government, more sharing of experience between parents, and more understanding and support from the wider community, parents will be better equipped to meet their first commitment, which has to be to their child.

Additional Reading

Adams, Jo, *Go Girls! Supporting Girls' Emotional Development and Building Self-esteem*, Sheffield: Centre for HIV and Sexual Health, 2002

Alexander, J., *Your Child Bullying: Practical and easy to follow advice*, Element Books, 1998

Bettelheim, Bruno, *A Good Enough Parent*, Thames and Hudson, 1989

Blake, Simon, and Brown, Rob, *Boys' Own: Supporting Emotional Resourcefulness and Self-esteem of Boys and Young Men*, Sheffield: Centre for HIV and Sexual Health, 2003

Clarke, Warren, 'The Dangers of Safe Play', *Recreation*, April 2003

Cleese, John, and Skynner, Robin, *Families and How to Survive Them*, Vermilion, 1993

Collins, Stephen, *Step-parents and their Children*, Souvenir Press, 1988

Faber, Adele, and Mazlish, Elaine, *Siblings without Rivalry*, Piccadilly Press, 1999

– *How to Talk so Kids will Listen and so Kids will Talk*, New York: Avon Books, 1982

– *Liberated Parents/ Liberated Children*, New York: Avon Books, 1975

Gerhardt, Sue, *Why Love Matters*, Routledge, 2004

Gill, Tim, 'Play, Child Care and the Road to Adulthood', *Children and Society*, Vol. 13, pp.67–9

Ginott, Haim, *Between Parent and Child*, New York: Macmillan, 1965

Goldstein, Sol, *Divorced Parenting*, Methuen, 1987

Hartley-Brewer, Elizabeth, *Self-esteem for Girls: 100 tips for raising happy and confident children*, Vermilion, 2000

– *Self-esteem for Boys: 100 tips for raising happy and confident children*, Vermilion, 2000

– *Raising a Self-starter*, MA: Da Capo Press, 2004

– *Talking to Tweenies: getting it right before it gets rocky with your eight- to twelve-year-old*, Hodder Mobius, 2004

Hayes, Eileen, *Encouraging Better Behaviour: A practical guide to positive Parenting*, NSPCC booklet, 2002

Hillman, Mayer (ed.), *Children, Transport and the Quality of Life*, PSI Publishing, 1993

– *One False Move: A Study of Children's Independent Mobility*, PSI Publishing, 1990

Kahn, Tim, *Bringing up Boys: a parents' guide*, Piccadilly Press, 1998

Leach, Penelope, *Getting Positive about Discipline: a guide for today's parents,* Barnardo's booklet, 1997

McNamara, Sarah, *Stress in Young People: What's new and what can we do?*, Continuum, 2000

Mullender, A., et al., *'Stop Hitting Mum!' Children Talk about Domestic Violence*, Young Voice, 2003

Neale, Bren, and Wade, Amanda, *Parent Problems!*

Children's views of life when parents split up, Young Voice, 2000

Open University, various study packs for parents offering guidance and understanding

Parker, Jan, and Stimpson, Jan, *Sibling Rivalry, Sibling Love*, Hodder Mobius, 2002

Steinem, Gloria, *Revolution from Within: A Book of Self-Esteem*, Bloomsbury, 1992

Wells, Rosemary, *Helping Children Cope with Divorce*, Sheldon Press, 1989

– *Helping Children Cope with Grief*, Sheldon Press, 1988

Wolfson, Richard, *Sibling Rivalry*, HarperCollins, 1995

Useful Organisations

SUPPORT FOR PARENTS

Crysis
BMCrysis, London, WC1B 3XX Tel: 020 7404 5011
Offers counselling advice if you feel your baby cries excessively.

Family Welfare Association
501 Kingsland Road, London, E8 Tel: 020 7254 6251
Aims to challenge the causes of poverty and to help meet the needs of families and children living in poverty.

Gingerbread
16–17 Clerkenwell Close, London, EC1R 0AA Tel: 020 7336 8183
A network of local self-help groups for single parents.

Home Start UK

2 Salisbury Road, Leicester, LE1 7QR Tel: 08000 686 368
Offers support, friendship and practical help in their own
homes to families with young children (under five) under
stress.

National Council for One-Parent Families

255 Kentish Town Road, London, NW5 2LX Tel: 020 7428
5400 Helpline: 0800 018 5026
Provides a free information service for lone parents, training
and consultancy services for lone parents and for employers
and professionals who work with them. NCOPF also acts as
a national voice for lone parents to government.

National Family and Parenting Institute

Unit 430, Highgate Studios, 53–79 Highgate Road, London,
NW5 1TL Tel: 020 7424 3460
www.nfpi.org www.e-parents.org

Newpin

Sutherland House, 35 Sutherland Square, London, SE17 3EE
Tel: 020 7703 6326
Provides support, group work, training and crèches to
families at risk of abusing or being abused.

Parenting Education and Support Forum

Tel: 020 7284 8370 Information Service: 020 7284 8389
www.parenting-forum.org.uk
Umbrella organisation that coordinates parenting education
initiatives and promotes standards and understanding.
Information service about support available nationwide for
parents.

Parentline Plus
Unit 520, Highgate Studios, 53–79 Highgate Road, London
NW5 1TL Tel: 020 7284 5500 National Helpline: 0808 800
2222 www.parentlineplus.org.uk

Stepfamily
Chapel House, 18 Hatton Place, London, EC1N 8RU Tel: 020
7372 0844
Provides information, newsletters, support and counselling
to members. There is a nationwide network of support
groups. Counselling telephone line (020 7372 0846) is
staffed by trained counsellors from 2–5 p.m. and 7–10 p.m.
every day.

PROTECTING CHILDREN'S INTERESTS

Child Poverty Action Group
94 White Lion Street, London, N1 9PF Tel: 020 7837 7979
Promotes action for the relief, directly or indirectly, of
poverty among children and families with children in the UK.

Childline
Helpline: 0800 1111

Kidscape Children's Charity
152 Buckingham Palace Road, London, SW1W 9TR Tel: 020
7730 3300
Teaches children about personal safety and preventing
abuse. Offers full teaching programmes, books for parents
and children, videos, free information leaflets and posters.
Also provides training in the form of its prevention and anti-
bullying programmes.

National Children's Bureau

8 Wakley Street, London, EC1V 7QE Tel: 020 7843 6000
Aims to identify and promote the interests of all children and to improve their status in a diverse society. Seeks to achieve this through research, policy development and the promotion of good practice in education, social work and health care.

NSPCC

42 Curtain Road, London, EC2A 3NH Tel: 020 7825 2500
Helpline: 0808 800 5000 www.nspcc.org.uk
Operates in England, Northern Ireland and Wales. See telephone directory for local branches. NSPCC aims to prevent child abuse in all forms and to give practical help to families with children at risk.

HELP WITH RELATIONSHIP PROBLEMS

London Marriage Guidance

76a New Cavendish Street, London, W1M 7LB Tel: 020 7580 1087
Offers a marital and couple counselling service to Inner London and the London area.

Marriage Counselling, Scotland

105 Hanover Street, Edinburgh, EH2 1DG Tel: 0131 225 5006
As above, for Scotland.

Relate (Marriage Guidance)

Herbert Gray College, Little Church Street, Rugby, CV21 3AP Tel: 01788 573241

Provides a completely confidential counselling service for relationship problems of any kind. Local branches are listed in the telephone directory under Relate.

PLAY

For information on play schemes in your area, contact the town hall or your local library.

Fair Play for Children in Scotland
Unit 29, 6 Harmony Row, Glasgow, G51 3BA Tel: 0141 425 1140
Voluntary organisation to promote and encourage play opportunities for children. Runs workshops for play leaders and local communities on play opportunities, e.g., traditional street games.

National Play Information Centre
199 Knightsbridge, London, SW7 1DE Tel: 020 7584 6464
Provides information about books and resources on play for children of all ages and local play facilities. Enquiries on all aspects of children's play welcome.

Woodcraft Folk
13 Ritherdon Road, London, SW17 8QE Tel: 020 8672 6031
An international organisation with no religious connections which coordinates children's weekly mixed clubs for boys and girls, with an outdoor focus.

FAMILY AND CHILDREN'S LEGAL RIGHTS

Children's Legal Centre
Wivenhoe Park, University of Essex, Colchester, Essex, CO4 3SQ Tel: 01206 872466
www.childrenslegalcentre.com

Family Rights Group
18 Ashwin Street, London, E8 3DL Tel: 020 7923 2628
Advice Line: 0800 731 1696
Advises parents, relatives or carers who have children in contact with social services departments or whose children are involved in child protection procedures.

National Family Mediation
Alexander House, Telephone Avenue, Bristol, BS1 5BS
Helpline: 0117 904 2825
www.nfm.u-net.com

PRE-SCHOOL EDUCATION

National Association for Gifted Children
Elder House, Milton Keynes, MK19 1LT Tel: 0870 770 3217
www.nagcbritain.org.uk
Offers support to parents and professionals and runs enrichment clubs through local branches for able children to attend, to help develop their potential. Pack for under-fives available.

Advisory Centre for Education (ACE)
www.ace-ed.org.uk

Pre-School Learning Alliance

69 King's Cross Road, London, WC1X 9LL Tel: 020 7833 0991 www.pre-school.org.uk

Represents and supports 15,000 community pre-schools in England and promotes the value of play. Hundreds of voluntary area organisers and branches nationwide. Parents' role considered crucial and their involvement in the child's pre-school experience is encouraged.

Young Minds

102–108 Clerkenwell Road, London, EC1M 5FA Tel: 020 7336 8445 Helpline: 0800 018 2138 www.youngminds.org

Index